THE QUEST FOR MEANING

A Journey Through Philosophy, the Arts, and Creative Genius

D1524415

William Cooney

University Press of America,® Inc.
Lanham • New York • Oxford

Copyright © 2000 by
University Press of America,® Inc.
4720 Boston Way
Lanham, Maryland 20706

12 Hid's Copse Rd.
Cumnor Hill, Oxford OX2 9JJ

Library of Congress Cataloging-in-Publication Data

Cooney, William
The quest for meaning : a journey through philosophy, the arts,
and creative genius/ William Cooney.
p.   cm.
Includes bibliographical references.
1.   Meaning (Philosophy) 2. Arts—Philosophy. I. Title.
B105.M4C66   1999   111'.85—dc21   99-048692 CIP

ISBN 0-7618-1526-0 (pbk: alk. ppr.)

This text is dedicated to the great philosopher Gabriel Marcel, an advocate for Being over Having, Participation over Spectatorship, Mystery over Problem, and most importantly, Hope over Despair. His theory of Creation, namely, that it is a reciprocal relationship between Giving and Receiving, is a much needed message in today's "Broken World."

Acknowledgements

I wish to thank the following for kind permission to use their works.

Harvard University Press:

The Poems of Emily Dickinson, and *The Letters of Emily Dickinson*:   Thomas H. Johnson, ed., Cambridge, Mass.: The Belknap Press of Harvard University Press, Copywright 1951, 1955, 1958, 1979, 1983, 1986 by the president and fellows of Harvard College.

Oxford University Press:

English Romantic Poetry and Prose: Russell Noyes, ed., Oxford University Press, New York, 1993.

Penguin Putnam Inc.:

The Picture of Dorian Gray: Oscar Wilde. Penguin Books, Canada, 1962 (foreword), 1983 (bibliography).

Contents

PART TWO: Profiles of Creative Genius

Preface

> *"Craving, constant craving, has always been."*
> —k.d. lang

In k.d. lang's wonderful song "Constant Craving," we encounter through music a theme which has been reflected in much of the art, literature and philosophy of the world. This theme centers on the essence of being a human person. The human person constantly craves after love, beauty, goodness and truth. The philosopher Aristotle, some 2300 years ago, used the word "potentiality" to describe this constant craving. In his view, we are all potentialities seeking fulfillment or "actualization." The seventeenth century philosopher Baruch Spinoza spoke of the "conatus"—the endeavor and desire of each individual to exist and to grow. In our own century, the psychologist Abraham Maslow has described "self-actualization" as the highest of all human needs, and the existentialist Gabriel Marcel wrote of the "need for Being" which he called the "ontological exigence." The ancient and modern religions of the world, too, recognize the striving after God, Being, Oneness and Completion. Science has also called attention to the seemingly built-in drive for existence on the part of the universe itself. The contemporary physicist and mathematician Roger Penrose, for example, has referred to this as the "intelligent groping" of the universe.

This book explores the "constant craving" which is, in short, our quest for meaning. We human persons are not content with just existing. We are the kind of creatures which need and even demand that existence have a purpose and a *logos*—i.e., a "reason why." This is the distinctive human feature. It is also why human existence can sometimes be forlorn. Meaning is not easy to achieve. We all strive after this fruit, but just as in the Greek myth of Tantalus, it is sometimes placed near enough to attract us, but far enough away to remain unpickable. Thus meaning tantalizes us all.

It is the thesis of this book that the arts can serve philosophy in its search after the fruit of meaning. It is that search, in fact, which gives birth to the arts in the first place. Thus the arts bear testimony to our "constant craving." A world without the arts, would be a world without that search; it would, in short, be a world without human persons, or, at least, a world in which no human person would wish to live. Such a world would be equivalent to Aldous Huxley's *Brave New World*—the "constant craving" would cease, and so would everything else which gives life its meaning. It would be a truly "absurd" world, as described by the 20th century philosopher and novelist Albert Camus. Such a world would be totally unresponsive to, in his words, "the wild longing for clarity whose call echoes in the human heart."

It is my hope that this book can serve as an aid to all those who feel that "constant craving" and "wild longing" of the human heart. For it is in having that feeling, I am convinced, that we become truly human.

William Cooney

Part One

Philosophy and the Arts

In part one we examine the philosophical and artistic ideas of Plato, Aristotle, Augustine, Aquinas, Leonardo, Michelangelo, Rousseau, Wordsworth, Coleridge, Shelley, Keats, Kierkegaard, Nietzsche, Marcel, Sartre, and the Postmodernists.

Chapter 1

Introduction: The Philosophical Attitude and the Gift of Existence

He who has a why can bear with almost any how.
—Friedrich Nietzsche

The only reality [for] an existing individual . . . is the fact that he exists; this reality constitutes his absolute interest.
—Søren Kierkegaard

Let us begin our quest with the consideration of a seemingly all too obvious but incredible truth— you and I exist. Let me repeat with emphasis, *you and I exist!* I think it will do us well to consider this truth for a moment. We spend the vast majority of our lives never contemplating this fact. We seem caught up in a world which has deprived us from considering it. Or, what is worse, *we seem constrained to take our existence for granted!*

I cannot think of anything more tragic and unfortunate than that. Our existence is wondrous and miraculous. We are the products of incredible and awesome forces. The various elements in the cosmos have, at some time in the vastly distant past, congealed into stars and from those great nuclear reactors has come life itself. This is no less remarkable whether it is attributable to the hand of God, or of Nature (or perhaps both, as Baruch Spinoza, 1632-1677, would have us believe, since for him God and Nature are one and the same—*Deus sive Natura*). Whether life has come from Divine Intelligence or from fortuitous circumstance does not seem to change the basic truth, i.e., *our existence is miraculous*. It seems that the consideration of our existence demands respect, reverence and thankfulness. What we are called to do, I believe, is to *think* about our existence. And, as Martin Heidegger (1889-1976) points out in his *What is Called Thinking?*, there may be a connection between *thinking* and *thanking*:

> *The Old English* thencan, *to think, and* thancian, *to thank, are closely related; the Old English noun for thought is* thanc *or* thonc—*a thought, a grateful thought, and the expression of such a thought* . . . . (WCT, 139)

This connection seems to find its way into colloquial language. In prayer, for example, we often say we are "giving thanks." To give thanks in this way is to deeply think (or meditate) about those aspects of our lives which are most precious to us and which give rise (or ought) to thankfulness.

In philosophical terms this attitude of respect, reverence, and thankfulness, is summed up in *wonder*. As Socrates (469-369 B.C.) said, "all philosophy begins in wonder." And it is specifically *wonder* that is called for rather than simple curiosity. Gabriel Marcel (1889-1973) helps us to see the difference between these two attitudes. Curiosity, he points out, is appropriate from the point of view of a *spectator* who is detached and uninvolved. But we human beings are not merely detached observers of life. We are *involved* in life. We are *within* existence and not at some vantage point outside it. We are *participants* in Being; we are not *homo spectans* but *homo particeps*.

Often we do not encounter the wonder of our own existence until life seems meaningless to us. This happens when life becomes a mere daily routine. Albert Camus (1913-1960) explains this in his famous *The Myth of Sisyphus*:

> *It happens that the stage sets collapse. Rising, streetcar, four hours in the office or the factory, meal, streetcar, four hours of work, meal, sleep, and Monday Tuesday Wednesday Thursday Friday and Saturday according to the same rhythm--this path is easily followed most of the time. But one day the "why" arises and everything begins in that weariness tinged with amazement.*
> (MS, 10)

"Weariness tinged with amazement"—this is the key. The "amazement" refers to the wonder of it all. The "weariness" refers to a level of uncomfortability. Marcel refers to this as a "metaphysical uneasiness," i.e., a feeling of personal crisis over the meaning of it all.

We have all experienced this question concerning the meaninglessness of our lives. It is important that we *feel* it. At the very least, it forces us to confront the fact of our existence. It wakes us up. More than 2500 years have passed since the Greek Presocratic thinker Heraclitus (c. 500 B.C.) made his famous distinction between those who are "awake" and those who are "asleep." And at roughly the same time, in India, the Buddha was calling for a level of "wakefullness." It seems that many of us are still asleep to the fact of our own existence. We too often live, it seems, in an artificial world. This is the world of Camus' streetcar, followed by four hours in the office, etc. In calling this world artificial, I do not mean to belittle or subtract from the importance of working life. Such a world can become artificial, however, when it forces us to so direct our lives towards the bottom line and the almighty dollar, that we have no time or energy left to *appreciate* our lives. In such a world, and with such an existence (in so far as it can be called an existence), we become prey to the kind of life that Henry David Thoreau (1817-1862) warned us of in his great *Walden*:

> *I went to the woods because I wished to live deliberately, to confront only the essential facts of life, and see if I could not learn what it had to teach, and not, when I came to die, discover that I had not lived.*
> (SWT, 304)

Should this not be our greatest fear—that we have not ever really lived? So many of us merely occupy a space and time, a frame of existence in a very unreal world. But when we are shaken up by the question of the meaning of it all, we enter into the *real* world of wonder. And when we focus on the meaning of our lives, our true *human journey* begins. Marcel, along with the great Franciscan theologian and saint Bonaventure (1221-1274), argued that we are all *homo viators*—wayfarers and travelers. The human being is an itinerant being. But the journey cannot begin if we are still asleep. We need to wake up! *You and I exist!*

And what do we encounter at the beginning of our journey? Nothing short of life itself. Life, that great gift and responsibility—for "to whom [this] is given, much is required." Everything, it seems, depends on the beginning. And life is rich enough to provide a marvelous beginning. But what of the responsibility? Wherein does it lie?

When we cease to take our lives for granted we are at the beginning stages of what I wish to call *the philosophical attitude*. This attitude begins when we *accept* our existence as a gift. Acceptance is no passive relation. It requires what Marcel calls an "active participation" on our part. The acceptance is necessary, because a gift is not a gift unless it is received. In a very important sense, the reception *creates* the gift. To receive the gift, I must open myself up to the gift. That is to say, *reception is also a giving.* You and I exist. Now we must actively open ourselves up to the reception of the gift. *We must, that is, become gifts ourselves.* And we must be gifts to each other, for it is not simply the case that *you* exist <u>and</u> *I* exist, but *we exist together.* Marcel helps us all to see that we are not solitary creatures. The ancient Greeks understood this. We are involved in each other's existence. The human being is a social being. As the great poet John Donne (1572-1631) has said,

No man is an island, entire of itself Every man is a piece of the continent, a part of the main. If a clod be washed away by the sea, Europe is the less, as well as if a promontory were, as well as if a manor of thy friend's or of thine own were. Any man's death diminishes me because I am involved in mankind, and therefore never send to know for whom the bell tolls; it tolls for thee.
(DEO, Med. XVII)

A Brief Hermeneutics on Related Concepts

In attempting to understand the human person's quest for meaning, we must first come to terms with what personhood itself is. Let us begin, therefore, to examine the concept of personhood through a brief hermeneutics of related ideas. *Hermeneutics* involves *interpretation* and exploration into the *original* and *basic meaning* of terms. Within the field of theology, for example, the hermeneutical method is used in an attempt to ascertain the meaning of the scriptures as can be derived from their original form in Hebrew or Greek. This method is used also in philosophy. Some notable thinkers like Heidegger, a famous existentialist thinker, have popularized the hermeneutical approach to *uncovering* the meaning of terms such as *truth, becoming,* and *being.* Indeed, Heidegger argues, a hermeneutics on the Greek word for "truth" (*aletheia*) itself, is enlightening. For *aletheia* means to be "uncovered," i.e., to be revealed. Understood in this light, hermeneutics is an approach to help uncover the meaning and to reveal the truths buried within concepts. Some very important things can be learned in this way. In the following, we explore some very basic terms related to the human person.[*]

Person

This term comes from the Latin *persona*, literally meaning "a mask." It was derived by the Romans most probably from the Etruscan civilization (one of the civilizations conquered by Rome) and their word *phersu*. For the Romans, in particular, the persona was often-times the mask that actors wore on the stage. The *persona*, therefore, refers to the character or part that one portrays in a play.

When we talk about the *human person*, then, how can this original meaning be applied? How does it fit? What does it reveal to us? Is there some sense in which to be a human person is, in effect, to play a part? Do we all, that is, wear the mask? And what is the mask used for? Is it, for example, an attempt to hide something? Is there some part (perhaps the deepest part) about ourselves as human persons that we would rather not reveal openly? May this have something to do with the great dictum of Socrates: "Know Thyself"? For is it not Socrates' intent for us to throw away the mask and reveal ourselves?

---

[*]All definitions utilized are from *Webster's New International Dictionary* and *Seventh New Collegiate Dictionary*.

These are evocative questions. The psychologist Carl Jung (1875-1961) explored these and related issues in his famous study into the *persona*. For him, the *persona* refers to an archetype that all humans share. In general, an archetype is a vestigial thought-pattern common to all humans. It is a universal part of the human make-up. For Jung, then, it is an essential part of what it means to be human. The human person is the one who hides; the one who wears the mask. And it is Jung along with his great teacher Sigmund Freud (1856-1939), who provides us with at least one most likely reason why we are the creature who wears the mask. I refer here to their famous investigations into the *Unconscious*, that great "hidden" part of who we are. The notion of the unconscious was not invented by Freud. It has its roots directly in such thinkers as Nietzsche, the father of atheistic existentialism. Freud greatly admired him, having once said that "Nietzsche had a more penetrating knowledge of himself than any other man who ever lived or was likely to live." And Jung, for his part, traces the notion of the unconscious to such philosophers as Gottfried Liebniz (1646-1716) and Immanuel Kant (1724-1804). Forerunners of the notion can be found, in fact, in the ancient Greek philosophers as well, and even farther back in the great religions and mythologies of the world. But Freud and Jung have greatly improved our understanding of the unconscious. For they provide the very likely reason for its existence. For the most part, it is the storage area for that information about ourselves that we would rather not reveal. Reveal, that is, not only to others, but even to ourselves: this takes us back to Socrates' evocation—"Know Thyself." The unconscious, that is, is a warehouse for truths that we have repressed because they are often too ugly for us to face up to. The mechanisms of repression and resistance, as outlined by Freud, are greatly at work here. It is much easier to wear the mask—to hide from those truths which surprise, embarrass, or even frighten us. The unconscious is that which the mask covers. And the unconscious is often controlled and characterized by "negative forces." This is what Plato (428-348 B.C.) called the "*Appetite*" (in several places in the *Republic*, he refers to it as the "beast"—that part of our souls which seeks immediate and complete satisfaction of desire). Freud called it the "*Id*" (the irrational, amoral motivation towards the pleasure principle). Nietzsche refers to it as the "*Dionysus*" in us all (the chaotic and frenzied life-force or stream of life in human nature). And Jung calls it the "*Shadow*" (the most primitive and animalistic feature of our personality).

This may not be the only clue, however. Hiddenness may not always be a sign of unwillingness to reveal ourselves. This is only, perhaps, the negative cause. Jung and Freud have given us one of the reasons which seems to explain why we hide. But there may be a more positive reason. And Jung, more so than Freud, seems to have been aware that the unconscious contained some healthy, positive and good contents as well. The unconscious is, perhaps, only part of the story. For it is not only the *human* person who hides. I refer here to what medieval Western (Jewish/Christian/Moslem) theologians referred to as the *Deus Absconditas*—The Hidden God. There is a sense, that is, of hiddenness in the *Ultimate Person*—God. This has been recognized by non-Western theologies as well. Hinduism uses the term *Maya* (Illusion), to talk (in so far as we *can* talk) about God—the Hidden Brahman-Atman. And what can explain this hiddenness? Surely, it cannot have the same kind of explanation. For can God be afraid to reveal the Godself? Are there truths about God's self that God is unwilling to admit to? Could God also benefit from Socrates' maxim? Does God have an unconscious side?

We seem to need a positive rather than a negative cause here. Might it not more simply be explained by the fact, also understood by Western and Eastern theologies alike, that the reason God is a *Deus Absconditas*, is because God is the *Infinite* Person while we who seek to know God, we human persons, are *finite* creatures? God is not fully knowable, then, not because God has something to hide—God does not wear the mask—but because of the Infinity of God's Being. The lesser cannot fully know the Greater. We who live in the realm of finity cannot comprehend Infinity. The imperfect cannot capture the Perfect.

But might there not be an analogue in the hiddenness of the *human* person as well? May there not be similar infinities in us as well? Could it be that the depth of our souls is also impenetrable? Like God, (to the extent that we are made in God's image— *Imago Dei*) that is, may our being also be overflowing and too full to be contained and too gigantic to be totally revealed?

Human, Man, Woman

When we search after the roots to be interpreted here, we find a cluster of notions. First, there is the Latin *homo*, from which a word like *homage* is derived. This is interesting. Is the human being that being which deserves homage or reverential regard? We may get a clue when we look at the roots of *man*, from the Latin *manus*=hand, but it may also be more akin to the ancient Sanskrit word *manu*, referring to a creature of special powers, special, that is, in comparison with the lower animal species. The *atman*, the Hindu reference to the soul itself, may also be connected here. The power of the human soul, especially concerning the higher intellectual abilities that *man* possesses, seems to be the justification for *homage*. The linguistic connections are not clear, but it is also interesting to note the Melanesian/Polynesian *mana*, which signifies the powerful forces of nature such as those embodied in the human being.

Yet *homo* is also linked to the Latin *humus*, from which the word *humble* is derived. This seems to reveal another side of who we are. On the one hand—with *homage*—we have in some sense a "superior" form of existence, on the other—with *humble*—we have a lowly form. In fact, *humus* literally refers to the earth, the soil (one should not fail to notice as well, that *manure* is a derivative of *man*). This seems to be a recognition of our source, i.e., the human creature has arisen out of the earth itself. This has obvious connections to both religion and science. I refer here to the "from dust to dust" notion found in the ancient scriptures of Judaism and Christianity (as well as to the ancient myths of Native American religion which also have the human species arising out of the earth itself), and to the theory of evolution.

We seem to arrive at an interesting *duality* (our high and low form). We shall encounter other dualities shortly. These dualities are among the many interesting features that hermeneutics can reveal to us. But before we move on, a small word of caution appears called for. For when we look at the roots of the word *woman*, for example, we see that it is derived from the Old English or Anglo-Saxon *man* + *wif* (wife). A woman, then, is a wife of a man. This seems to a rather sexist kind of definition. The cultures which gave forth such a word were certainly male-dominated societies and this is revealed in their language as well as in their law, politics and religion (indeed, everywhere). This example indicates that original root meanings sometimes reveal more than just simple truths. They also make plain the various prejudices of a culture, and we must keep on our guard concerning these.

Soul, Spirit, Psyche

The word *soul,* derived from the Middle English original word *soule,* is traced to the Germanic/Icelandic languages with words like *seele* and *sala.* The precise origin and meanings have been lost. A more direct connection is found in the way *soul* is defined. It refers to the *spiritual* element found within the human being. And so we turn to the word for spirit, which is the Latin *spiritus,* literally "breath." The spirit, then, is the *breath of life.* This, again, has connections to religious ideas. Here we need only remember that God breathed life into the nostrils of Adam (from the Hebrew *Adamah,* meaning soil or earth; thus some theologians infer that "Adam" refers not simply to one distinct individual, but to the human species as a whole; i.e., the earthly creature made in the image of God). The Hebrew *nepesh* (meaning soul), seems also to carry this notion of the Divine breath of life. The Sanskrit, likewise, uses *babhasti*="he blows," to speak of the soul. The Greek *psyche,* too, reflects this meaning, from *psychein*="to breath, blow or cool." *Psyche* is, of course, the basis of our word "psychology"—the study of the mind (as in the contemporary science), or more widely, the investigations of the soul (we refer to Aristotle's study of the soul, for example, as his "psychology"). *Psyche* is also represented in Greek Mythology, as the personification of soul—a beautiful maiden endowed with the wings of a butterfly, meant to symbolize immortality. The *psyche*, then, is that immortal and divine spark within us all: all *human* beings, that is. The Greeks also recognized lower forms of *psyche* in non-human (sub-human) life forms. Both Plato and Aristotle refer to the *rational psyche* (belonging to the human being), the *animal psyche* (belonging to lower animals), and the *vegetative psyche* (belonging to the plant kingdom). Like the Latin word *anima* (soul), which refers to the vital principle—in short, life itself, *psyche* refers in general to the very breath of life itself, and that the human being possesses a specific (no doubt, divine) type of *psyche*.

Self, Individual

The term "self" stems from the Anglo-Saxon *self, seolf, sylf*, and refers to having a single nature or character. It points to the quality of being unmixed and selfsame. It denotes also the quality of being undivided—as hinted at in the word "individual." The "individual," from the Latin *individuus* (meaning not divisible), along with "self," calls to mind a sense of the self or individual as a person in their unique, separate and distinct state. This is what we mean when we say of someone, for example, that they are (or are not) being their "true selves." It was this state of being a self that Socrates' great dictum (Know thyself) seems to call us towards. A person who is a self, in this sense, is a person who stands out from the crowd—s/he is a true individual, not merely a member of the herd. This is clearly what Soren Kierkegaard (1813-1855), the father of Religious

Existentialism, had in mind when he called for each person to become an existing individual, taking personal responsibility for their own beliefs and actions, rather than "hiding" in the crowd.

Reflections on the Human Person as Duality

Among the many things we learn from our short hermeneutics, is the *duality* that is often inherent within the basic descriptive terms we use to talk about the human person. There is the duality of the homage/humble, as discussed above. There also seems to be a duality of high and low when we consider that the human person is seen to have some share in the divine *psyche* or *anima* (and therefore has a "high" feature), but also, the human shares an earthly form—from *humus*—(and therefore a "low" feature). We are, in a sense, paradoxical creatures. We have both god-like and animal-like characteristics. This odd quality of the human being is examined in such notions as Thomas Aquinas' (1225-1274) great "Chain of Being." For St. Thomas, the human being occupies the highest realm of material creation—we are at the summit of earthly existence. But humans are also spiritual creatures. We occupy the bottom ranks, however, within that world.   According to Aquinas, in fact, it is precisely *because* we occupy the lowest regions of spirit, that we need a physical body which can enable our lowly spirits to do their work.

There   is   also   the   duality   of   the hidden/unhidden features of our personality as we have briefly seen. We shall come back to this theme again and again. It seems to me that the arts, literature and film reveal both the masks that we wear and, at their best, what is under the mask. The arts, therefore, get at the truth in a literal way, i.e., recalling Heidegger's hermeneutics on "truth" (*aletheia*)=to become uncovered or revealed.

But there are other dualities hinted at by our short treatment. There is the dark side of our personalities (Plato's "appetite," Freud's "id," Nietzsche's "dionysus," etc.), which implies a bright side (indeed, the same thinkers had names for this too—Plato's "reason," Freud's "ego," and Nietzsche's "apollo"). This contrast reveals both negative and positive forces working within us and warring with each other. The notion of opposing forces has been recognized by many ancient cultures in their native religions and philosophies. The Presocratic philosophers (6th c. B.C.) pointed to it. But it is perhaps best portrayed in the great symbol from Taoism—China's oldest native religion. I am referring to the great *Yin and Yang* as illustrated here.

This symbol explores the deeply hidden relationship with the universe (both the macro-universe, or the cosmos itself, and the micro-universe that each human being comprises). Long before physics was to come to terms with this truth, Taoism was teaching that reality is somehow the holding together of positive (yang) and negative (yin) forces. In an exploration of the yin and yang, we also come to learn a very important truth, i.e., the necessity of each side. For the yin is not "negative" in the sense of being bad or evil. Nor is the yang "positive" in the reverse sense. *What is bad or evil is the disharmony of the two. Goodness=harmony, balance, equilibrium.* This great truth was recognized, as we shall see, by thinkers from Aristotle (the Doctrine of the Golden Mean), to Nietzsche and Jung. Other religions of the world, too, have recognized it, as in the great teachings in India of the Buddha (the Middle Path) and Confucius (the Doctrine of the Mean), his contemporary in China.

This notion is deeply explored, as well, in Hinduism's triadic understanding of God as *Brahma*—the Creator, *Shiva*—the Destroyer, and *Vishnu*—the Preserver. The role of Shiva is most familiar in portrayals of the great cosmic dance as pictured below.

In the great cosmic dance, Shiva, the many-handed god, holds both a drum which beats the sound of creation, and fire, which signals the coming destruction. But it is important that we see that Shiva's destructive role is *not* interpreted as evil. For in destroying the world, Shiva makes a new one possible, born out of the ashes of the old. The cosmos must, in the tradition of Hinduism, go through successive reincarnations. It is interesting to note that many contemporary astrophysicists, Carl Sagan, for example, believe that Hinduism has hit upon a most likely cosmological theory. In his *Cosmos*, he explains this in the following way:

> *The Hindu religion is the only one of the world's great faiths dedicated to the idea that the Cosmos itself undergoes an immense, indeed an infinite, number of deaths and rebirths. . . . These profound and lovely images are, I like to imagine, a kind of premonition of modern astronomical ideas. Very likely, the universe has been expanding since the Big Bang, but it is by no means clear that it will continue to expand forever. [It may] partake of a very Indian succession of cycles, expansion followed by contraction, universe after universe. If we live in such an oscillating universe, then the Big Bang is not the creation of the Cosmos, but merely the end of the previous cycle, the destruction of the last incarnation of the Cosmos.*
> (C, 258-259)

Sagan's words indicate, among other things, something which is often overlooked, i.e., science and religion are not always at odds. Sometimes the two achieve the same truths.

It seems that in each one of us there exists the *yin and yang; shiva and vishnu.* The microcosm appears to mirror the macrocosm. Each of us is a universe, though not, as we have said, self-contained and isolated (remember Marcel and Donne). The human universe is a shared experience. This is why we must explore it together—*You and I exist.*

Selected Bibliography for Chapter One

Camus, Albert: *The Myth of Sisyphus and Other Essays.* Random House, New York, 1955. Abbreviated (MS).

Cooney, William: *Reflections on Gabriel Marcel.* The Edwin Mellen Press, Lewiston-Queenston-Lampeter, 1989.

Donne, John: *Devotions Upon Emergent Occasions, Meditation XVII,* printed in Witherspoon, Alexander (ed.), *Seventeenth-Century Prose and Poetry.* Harcourt, Brace and World, New York, 1963. Abbreviated (DEO).

Heidegger, Martin: *What is Called Thinking?* (trans.) J. Glenn Gray. Harper Torchbooks, New York, 1968. Abbreviated (WCT).

Noss, John B. and David S.: *Man's Religions.* Macmillan Press, New York, 1984.

Sagan, Carl: *Cosmos.* Random House, New York, 1980. Abbreviated (C).

Thoreau, Henry David: *Walden,* as printed in *The Selected Works of Thoreau.* Houghton Mifflin, Boston, 1975. Abbreviated (SWT).

Chapter 2

The Nature, Tasks and Branches of Philosophy

In order to become better acquainted with the discipline of philosophy itself, let us now more deeply and specifically examine its nature, tasks and branches. Once Linus overheard Charlie Brown, that great cartoon character and sometime philosopher, engaged in the following conversation with himself (Charlie, like the rest of us, sometimes talks to himself): "Who am I? What am I? What should I do? That's philosophy!" To this Linus replied, "sounds like amnesia to me!"

Linus' attitude, I am afraid, is shared by many, especially outside of the academic world. People just don't know what to do with philosophy. It conjures up for them all sorts of images for people, from the Druids and ancient astronauts, to Shirley Maclaine and discussions of reincarnation and channeling. Her books, after all, are often strategically displayed next to such classics in philosophy as Jean Paul Sartre's *Being and Nothingness* and Bertrand Russell's *History of Western Philosophy* in mall bookstores across the country.

And Linus' attitude, I am even more afraid, sometimes spills over into the academic world as well. Even some college professors (non-philosophers) are unsure about what philosophy is or what it should be doing. This is often based in a misunderstanding concerning the nature and tasks of philosophy. There are even some, both in and outside of academia, who believe that philosophy is simply an out-dated hold-over from the ancient past, that is to say, an anachronism. Their argument goes something like this: "philosophy was useful one day, before people really knew what they were doing. This was a time when abstraction and generality were acceptable. But ever since we began to specialize, philosophy has been losing ground. Medicine was the first to splinter off, then, slowly but surely the other sciences found their own homes."

This attitude, let us call it the "anachronism argument," has some historical antecedents. Regarding this connection, it rightly refers to the fact that at one time all (or nearly all) disciplines were considered branches of philosophy. The sciences were simply inquiries into the "philosophy of nature," for example, and psychology was "philosophy of mind." A holdover of this is recognized when we see that one can earn a "Ph.D" in biology, chemistry, psychology, art, music, english, etc. "Ph.D" abbreviates "Doctorate in the Philosophy of . . . ." But these separate disciplines, according to the anachronism argument, have become specialized and distinct from philosophy.

Even some very good philosophers, albeit unwittingly, seem to lend their support for this kind of argument by suggesting that philosophy is just the sum of all the special sciences. This is based, I believe, on Rene Descartes' (1596-1650) famous metaphor of philosophy as a tree; metaphysics being the roots, physics the trunk, and the special sciences its branches. William James (1842-1910), for example, seems to have thought that philosophy could fully dissolve into the individual sciences. And Bertrand Russell (1872-1970) has said that "every advance in knowledge robs philosophy of some problem which formerly it had."

Is philosophy the discipline which slowly digs its own grave? As it gives birth to its offspring (medicine, physics, psychology, etc.) does it thereby become less and less fertile and useful? Is there now, since specialization seems almost complete, nothing left for philosophy to do? *What good is philosophy, anyway?* Consider my own personal case. When I teach introduction to philosophy, I tell my students that what philosophy concerns itself with are the fundamental issues of the *self*, the *cosmos* around us, and with *God*. But could it not be argued that these three areas are now the territories of other, more specialized disciplines? Is not the self the province of psychology?, the cosmos the property of physics?, and God the domain of theology? In short, has philosophy finally been nudged out?

The answer, thankfully, is an indefatigable NO! We need not be convinced by the anachronism argument, because it is based in several fallacies. First, it makes the faulty assumption that the same content cannot be studied by more than one discipline. The fallacy occurs in believing that all of the special sciences have claimed "dibs" on the various subject areas. But the areas of self, cosmos and God, are really too vast for any one discipline to deplete. Second, and more important, the anachronism argument errors in thinking that a discipline is only defined by its association with a content. Art and medicine, however, are both interested in the intricacies of human anatomy, but this does not make them alike as disciplines. Their differences lie, rather, in the *mode* of interest each has, and the *method* each uses to explore that interest. Medicine's method is to use the information gained towards perfecting ways of preventing illness. Art's method is to become familiar with the human anatomy, so that artistic works can be more soundly based. *A discipline, therefore, is distinctive not so much due to the particular subject area it studies, but according to the way in which it studies it, and the goals which direct that study.* The anachronism argument is wrong in identifying philosophy with content areas in the first place. Philosophy should not be so closely associated with subject areas that it becomes defined by that association. By analogy, the situation is quite like the aging parents whose children have all grown up and moved away. If the parents have an identity crisis, it is because they have made the mistake of identifying themselves too fully with their children in the first place. Philosophy, like those aging parents, need not make that mistake.

I have become convinced that philosophy is best characterized by its mood or spirit. In the end, philosophy is cast in the interrogative mood rather than the declarative. Philosophy is not so much in the business of providing answers as it is in the promotion of investigation and exploration. It is more concerned with the *human journey* itself, than with captured territory. "Who am I? What am I? What should I do?" *Charlie Brown was right. These are the questions of philosophy.* And if to us, like Linus, it sounds like amnesia, it is only because we too often avoid asking these questions seriously enough. It is the difficult and important task of philosophy to help us all ask these questions more seriously.

In this book we attempt to explore the quest for meaning. We human beings seem to be unique in that we call our own being into question. That is to say, we seek to know who and what we are. Heidegger suggests that it is this feature which distinguishes us from all other animals. Namely, our own being is an issue for us. We are the creatures which *wonder* about our own existence. We want to know, as Heidegger has stated it, "why there is something rather than nothing." We are the kind of creature which seeks not only life, but a meaningful life. It was Socrates who said that "the unexamined life is not worth living." We human beings seek the examined/meaningful life more so than even life itself.

Philosophy, then, is that discipline which examines life. Though there are many issues that philosophers examine, that examination centers itself around five major areas (with many subdivisions)— these are the major branches of philosophy.

Branches of Philosophy

LOGIC concerns itself with the study of correct forms of reasoning. It makes distinctions between types of reasoning such as deductive (claims of certainty) and inductive (claims of probability) thinking. It can become a very advanced study into the formal rules of logic (symbolic logic), or focus on the informal elements of language itself and the fallacious arguments which often arise therein.

EPISTEMOLOGY deals with the area of knowledge claims (*episteme* is Greek for "knowledge"). It seeks to discover just what can be known with certainty by human beings and what can never be known at all. Issues such as the limitations of the human mind, and the nature of the mind itself become prominent here.

METAPHYSICS focuses in on existence or being itself. It concentrates on such questions as the nature of the self, the world in general, and on the questions concerning the nature and existence of God. It also becomes involved in more particular philosophical controversies such as the freedom/determinism debate.

ETHICS asks questions concerning good and bad forms of behavior. It seeks not merely to describe but to prescribe good/ethical behavior. In that sense, this branch is a *normative* discipline (it seeks to establish and promote norms). Ethics can obviously invite us to consider very many controversial issues concerning values.

AESTHETICS also concerns itself with values, though it deals with the artistic rather than the moral values. It seeks to discover what the essence of beauty is. What makes a work of art beautiful? What is good vs. bad art, in so far as we can distinguish these?

The Relationship Between Truth and Beauty

There are very many issues and sub-issues that arise within the branches of philosophy. There are also, of course, many areas of overlap in the mix. Since this book seeks out the aid provided by the arts, literature and film, aesthetics will often come into play. In general, we wish to discover what these aesthetic enterprises can teach us about the human condition. And there is some reason to believe that the arts can reveal truths to us. I am referring to the long-held belief about the deep relationship between beauty and truth. To the scientist, this truism is well known. It gives rise to the famous "Ockham's Razor" (named after William of Ockham (c.1280-1349), the famed medieval philosopher), which states that truth is linked with simplicity (beauty). When deciding between competing theories, for example, Ockham's Razor is our scientific guide. A famous example of this is the debate, at the beginnings of the Renaissance, concerning Ptolemy's (2nd century A.D.) geocentric theory (earth-centered universe) versus Copernicus' (1473-1543) heliocentric theory (sun-centered theory). Which is the true picture of our universe? Copernicus' view won out, at least in part, because of Ockham's Razor. It required none of the "ugly" ellipses (wanderings) of the planets that would be required if the Ptolemaic system were to be accepted. The same or similar principle is often utilized in the fields of mathematics and physics as well. Those mathematical theories which explain the greatest amount of physical facts are touted as "truer" pictures, when they have an aspect of aesthetic beauty. Such an example comes to mind, for instance, when we consider Einstein's famous conjectures related to his proposed theories of relativity—"They must be true" he said, "because they are so beautiful."

The connection between truth and beauty is often recognized in the humanities as well. Consider, for example, the famous (and somewhat controversial[*]) last lines from the *"Ode on a Grecian Urn,"* written by Romantic poet John Keats' (1795-1821):

> *Beauty is truth, truth beauty,—that is all*
> *Ye know on earth, and all ye need to know.*

Taken literally, Keats' words suggest not only a connection, but an identification between beauty and truth. Such an identification is often suggested by the so-called "art for art's sake" philosophy, which claims that art (which arrives at beauty) has its own inner truth.

Other poets direct our attention to the connection between truth and beauty. One

---

[*]Keats scholars disagree concerning the precise meaning of these lines and whether, among other things, the lines should be in quotation.

marvelous portrayal is found in the following poem from Emily Dickinson (1830-1886):

> *I died for Beauty—but was scarce*
> *Adjusted in the Tomb*
> *When One who died for Truth, was lain*
> *in an adjoining Room—*
>
> *He questioned softly "Why I failed"?*
> *"For Beauty", I replied—*
> *"And I—for Truth—themself Are One—*
> *We Brethren, are", He said—*
>
> *And so, as Kinsmen, met a Knight—*
> *We talked between the Rooms—*
> *Until the Moss had reached our lips—*
> *And covered up—our names—*

Within this wonderful poem we encounter the basic theme of this text. The connection between truth and beauty is held to as a basic intuition. It is, as Aristotle refers to such matters, a "first principle." The truth of such principles cannot be demonstrated. To demonstrate them, they would have to become conclusions based on some previous principles. But then they would not be first principles, but principles of the second and third order. Such principles cannot be understood save through an interior intuition. Such truths are deeply and personally *felt*, rather than publicly provable through the reason alone.

This text focuses in on the *personal, human journey*. It calls upon the reader to *feel truths* such as the relationship between beauty and truth. This is chiefly why we seek the aid of the arts, for they help us to feel the truth. In the end, we seek out those truths which can be felt rather than simply thought in the mood of curiosity. Truths that can be felt, "subjective truths," as Kierkegaard called them, are much more important to humans than so-called "objective" truths. In speaking about this distinction, Kierkegaard makes the following claims:

> *The thing is to find a truth which is true for me, to find the idea for which I can live and die. What would be the use of discovering so-called objective truth, of working through all systems of philosophy and of being able, if required, to review them all and show up the inconsistencies within each system; . . . . What good would it do me if truth stood before me, cold and naked, not caring whether I recognized her or not, and producing in me a shudder of fear rather than a trusting devotion?*
> (K, 5)

In looking for "the truth which is true for me" we seek the "why" of our existence. This is the "why" which Friedrich Nietzsche (1844-1900) refers to—"He who has a why can bear with almost any how." It is the "why" which breaks into the artificial world of the daily routine pointed to by Camus. And it is the "why" which gives birth to the feeling and experience of wonder.

This takes us back to our discussions concerning wonder. *To wonder*, it seems to me, *involves us much more in a feeling than a thought.* But it is also a feeling which can be greatly aided by thought. Thought is a friend, not an enemy.

We turn next, to thoughts on the nature of philosophy and its relationships to the arts, as expressed by the two men who are the most pivotal thinkers from the Ancient period in the West—Plato and Aristotle.

Selected Bibliography for Chapter Two

Dickinson, Emily: Poem #445, as printed in Johnson, Thomas; *Emily Dickinson: An Interpretive Biography.* Belknap Press of Harvard University, Cambridge, Mass., 1955.

Kaufmann, Walter: *The Portable Nietzsche.* The Viking Press, New York, 1954.

Keats, John: "*Ode on a Grecian Urn,*" printed in *The Norton Anthology of English Literature* (3rd. ed.). W.W. Norton and Co., New York, 1974.

Kierkegaard, Soren: Journal entry dated August 1, 1835, printed in Bretall, Robert (ed.), *A Kierkegaard Anthology.* Modern Library, New York, 1946. Abbreviated (K).

Kirk, G.S., and Raven, J.E.: *The Presocratic Philosophers.* Cambridge University Press, London, 1957.

Stumpf, Samuel Enoch: *Socrates to Sartre* (5th ed.). McGraw Hill, New York, 1993.

Chapter 3

Plato:
Philosophy and the Arts,
and the Need for Control

Plato is philosophy and philosophy is Plato.
—Ralph Waldo Emerson

As we can tell from Emerson's line above, Aristocles (427-347 B.C.), who was called "Plato" (according to some, because of his broad shoulders and frame) was one of the foremost thinkers in the world. The great 20th century mathematician and philosopher Alfred North Whitehead also recognized Plato's enormous importance when he wrote that all of philosophy is merely a "series of footnotes to Plato."

It is difficult to summarize all of Plato's accomplishments and influences. One of the reasons for his acclaim is that he was one of the first to offer a complete and unified system of thought. Philosophy began in Greece around 600 B.C. with the *Presocratics* (philosophers before Socrates) such as Thales and Anaximander, who concentrated their efforts around the understanding of the physical world of nature (*physis*). These first philosophers were primarily cosmologists investigating the origins, nature, and end of the *cosmos* (universe) itself. One of the greatest of these thinkers was Democritus (c.460-360 B.C.), for example, who is the father of atomic theory. Socrates shifted the focus of philosophy from a concern about the physical world to one centered around the human person, in particular, to the nature of the soul (*psyche*), and how one should achieve a just and good life. Thus some contend that Socrates is rightly called the father of psychology (the study of *psyche*), and others, more daringly, suggest that he invented the concept of the soul itself. This last contention is no doubt exaggerated since the subject of the soul had, long before Socrates, been the province of the world's great faiths, as we have seen in such examples as the Hebrew *nepesh*, the Hindu *babhasti*, the Buddhist *atman*, etc. But Socrates is to be given credit for the shift in philosophy's concentration from *physis* to *psyche*. More simply put, Socrates brought one branch of philosophy to the forefront, namely ethics, understood as the investigation into the just and good life, in short, how one should live.

Socrates' life (469-399 B.C.) and teachings had tremendous impact on Plato. Most importantly, Plato became attracted to Socrates' search for real, eternal truths (Justice, Beauty, Goodness) which had an existence beyond the mere physical world of flux and change. And like most young Athenians of his time, he was impressed too with the life and character of the man himself. Socrates was a brave soldier who had defended Athens often in times of war, but he was also considered to be "the wisest man in Athens," and by many "the most just." This made it all the more difficult for Plato and others of like admiration when Socrates was brought up on charges of impiety and corrupting the minds of the youth. He was tried and executed by his own state of Athens, and ordered to drink the hemlock (a poison which slowly invades the bloodstream) in 399 B.C. This event disturbed many throughout Greece. Plato in particular was motivated by this grave tragedy to give up on his earlier political aspirations (his bloodlines were thoroughly aristocratic and could be traced back to Solon, the original lawgiver of ancient Greece). Plato took up the mission of Socrates, and in his great *Dialogues* he develops his own ideas taken from Socrates' lead.

Plato is also considered by many to be the western world's first great educator, since he started what is thought to be the first school in the west which he called *The Academy* (after the mythic figure Academus—this is where we get our word for "academics"). There one could learn from the masters in philosophy, mathematics and the physical sciences. This school remained open for more than 900 years, being closed by the Emperor Justinian in A.D. 529. In its beginnings this school provided an opportunity for the young intellectuals of Greece. The greatest of these young students was none other than Aristotle who there began to shape his own thinking, a thinking which was later to rival Plato's own monumental effort. More about Aristotle later.

Another major impact from Plato concerns his influence on religion. His ideas played a major role in the Christian world, for example, chiefly through the great Saint Augustine (354-430), who used the Platonic world of the Forms or Ideas (those universal, eternal and unchangeable realities) as the bridge to knowledge of God. Who else, reasoned Augustine, could be the source of eternal and unchangeable realities, if not an eternal and unchangeable Being?

Plato's View Concerning The Impact of the Arts on the Development of the Human Person

The thesis of this text is that the human quest for meaning is both aided by and reflected in the arts as they are created and experienced by persons. In this section, therefore, we will explore Plato's view concerning the arts and their impact. As an educator, Plato was greatly aware of the importance of the arts. He was among the first, in fact, to duly recognize the tremendous influence the arts can have on the development of human character. In his *Republic*, Plato's dialogue concerning how to best organize a just society, he argues that in a just educational system we must have "gymnastic for the body" and "music for the soul." He continues to express this view with the following question concerning why the musical arts are so important:

> [I]s it not for this reason . . . that education in music is most sovereign, because more than anything else rhythm and harmony find their way to the inmost soul and take strongest hold on it, bringing with them and imparting grace, if one is rightly trained, and otherwise the contrary? (R, 401 d-e)

We find expressed in this question the power of music, surely, but also the potential danger ("and otherwise the contrary"). Plato was aware, then, of the potential for the arts to "rightly" educate our young, but he was also aware of the need for some control. He was firmly convinced, like many parents in the present day, that not all musical art is equally harmonious and good for the soul. There were particular modes of music, in fact, that Plato warned against, saying that "gracelessness and evil rhythm are akin to evil speaking and the evil temper . . . ." The questions often raised in our own time, then, concerning potential harmful effects of certain forms of music or of certain contents, are Platonic concerns.

In order to understand these and other of Plato's views regarding the importance of the arts, indeed, his *Aesthetics* in general, we must first briefly describe Plato's *Metaphysics* and *Epistemology* (his view of reality and how knowledge of reality is possible), and finally, his *Ethics* and *Psychology* in particular. All of these areas are inevitably intertwined for Plato.

Plato's METAPHYSICS centered around the doctrine of the Forms or Ideas (from the Greek: *Eidos*) which he believed to be the only ultimately real substances. Everything else and the physical world in general was seen as merely a copy and therefore less real. Reality lies in Form and Idea. That which is fully real is universal and unchanging, while the physical world is characterized by change. Plato offers us a dualism, i. e., there are two worlds; the physical world of appearances and opinion, and the world of the immaterial Ideas—the only truly real world—which is the realm of the mind and of knowledge. As an example, Plato argues that particular things in the world, for example, particular beautiful things (a beautiful horse, or human being), or even more or less good things (a healthy person), are merely instances of the commonly shared universal characteristic (Beauty or Goodness in and of themselves) which is the reality each participates in. It is this universal which is the truly existing essence (of Beauty or Goodness). The individual instance is changeable. The particular examples fade away and cease to be beautiful or good. The essences themselves, however, are changeless and remain as the standard and form for all those particulars who share in them.

The Platonic metaphysics can become extremely difficult and controversial. Just what exactly are these Forms or Ideas? In what sense do they exist? Where do they exist? What is the precise relationship between them and the particular instances of them? All of these questions were raised by Plato himself, and they continue to vex any comfortable Platonist. For our part, we can understand Plato's thinking best when we compare it on the one hand to the science of mathematics, which does study the abstract, mental entities such as the concept of triangularity, for example, as opposed to any particular drawing of a triangle on the chalkboard. Triangularity stands as the standard and essence or pattern that must be represented by any particular example. Plato's attraction to mathematics as the best model for true understanding was centered around his conviction, as expressed by contemporary mathematicians Philip Davis and Reuben Hersh, that

> [T]he mission of philosophy was to discover true knowledge behind the veil of opinion and appearance, the change and illusion of the temporal world. In this task, mathematics had a central place, for mathematical knowledge was the outstanding example of knowledge independent of sense experience, knowledge of eternal and necessary truths. (TME, 325)

Plato's view of the nature of mathematics (which has many advocates such as Roger Penrose, but also has some critics) and his attraction to it, accounts for the sign said to hang above the entrance to the great Academy—"Let no one ignorant of geometry enter here."

In attempting to come to grips with Plato's metaphysics, one can also think, on the other hand, of the major theme found in religion, namely its insistence that this particular physical world is only part of reality. The other, more important, part is the spiritual world of God which lies behind the physical world of appearance and change. In the end most interpreters of Plato agree that in his philosophy we encounter a religious metaphysics and that the world of the Forms or Ideas, the only true realities for Plato, are indeed those which inhabit the spiritual world having God as their source.

In considering Plato's EPISTEMOLOGY, or his theory of knowledge, one needs to keep the metaphysics in mind. To truly *know* something (as opposed to merely having an opinion or belief), one must focus on the universal essence of a thing rather than simply deal with the particular instance. One who really knows what beauty is, for example, focuses not solely on this or that example, but on the common essence of beauty that each particular example shares in. For Plato, then, true knowledge focuses away from this physical, changeable world to the other—more real—world of changeless Form and Idea. And the mind which comes to know the Forms, is no empty slate, no *tabula rasa*. The mind, he believed, is in fact in possession of truth already, though only in latent form. The human mind has, so to speak, innate ideas of truth which are brought out in clearer light before the mind's eye, during reason and dialogue.

Finally, in looking at Plato's ETHICS and PSYCHOLOGY we are presented with a rich and penetrating discussion of the nature of the *psyche* itself, and of the just and healthy *psyche* or character. For Plato, as with Socrates before him, justice is a harmony of disparate elements. The just and ethical society, for example, is one in which all the various elements work hand in hand together (the rulership, the guardian and the craftsmen classes). Society or the State is, in Plato's view, "man writ large." What we easily see reflected on this larger scale, also exists in each individual. In the *Republic* and the *Phaedrus* Plato sees the *psyche* (soul, mind, or personality) as being composed of three major components. These three are *Reason*, which gives the *psyche* its rational, analytic, and logical capacities; the *Appetite*, which impels the *psyche* towards the satisfaction of basic desires (food, sex, etc.), and *Spirit*, which acts as a form of conscience and works along with the reason to bring the appetite under control. In his *Phaedrus*, Plato beautifully expresses the inter-workings of the *psyche* in a metaphor likening it to the powers of a team of winged horses and their winged charioteer. The charioteer represents reason, the element of control and direction. The two steeds are likened to the appetite—the unruly horse constantly attempting to stir off course so that basic desires can be met, and the spirit—the noble horse of "good stock" which serves as a natural ally to the reason to help bring the unruly horse back into line. In the *Republic* we learn that the appetite is "the largest part of the soul" and therefore that neither the reason nor spirit working alone can restrain it. What is required is that the reason rule the *psyche* by making use of the spirited element, working as a team to bring things under control. The healthy and just soul is the one which learns to harmonize these various elements, and

Plato's psychological theory has gone on to influence our view of the *psyche*, indeed, it had a major impact on Sigmund Freud's famous theories concerning *Id*, *Ego* and *Superego*. Furthermore, many scientists now contend a view of brain structure which in large measure supports the Platonic view of a tripartite *psyche*. A current theory known as the "triune brain," for example, is espoused by such researchers and scientists as Paul MacLean and Carl Sagan. This view sees the brain as divided between the "reptilian complex"—the brain stem and the oldest and deepest layer (this seems to match with Plato's "appetite" which is the oldest and strongest part of the psyche), the "limbic system"—the mammalian portion and that area of the brain, some contend, which is the seat of the emotions and compassionate behavior (this can be likened to Plato's "spirited element"), and the "neocortex"—the newest and primate portion which accounts for higher forms of functioning such as the capacity for reason (this can be clearly associated with Plato's "reason"). Indeed, in his *The Dragons of Eden*, Sagan has argued that Plato's tripartite charioteer metaphor, is a "superior agreement" (i. e., more accurate than Freud's id, ego, superego) when it is compared with current brain research.

Plato's Critique of the Arts

Having reviewed these areas in Plato's philosophy, let us now see how each impacts on his view of art. We shall find that all of these concerns; the metaphysical, epistemological, ethical and psychological, will point up difficulties within the arts and the role they play in our society.

Plato's Metaphysics:
Art does not bring us in touch with reality

For Plato art can be considered at the third remove from truth and reality because it imitates and copies the physical world which, in turn, is a copy of the real world of the Forms. Plato is chiefly talking here about the "mimetic" (imitating) arts such as painting, but also includes those makers of tragedy who intend simply to imitate events in history. He is aware that there are other, non-imitative, forms of art and that not all tragedy is imitative

Plato's Epistemology:
Art does not bring us knowledge

Because art does not bring us in touch with reality it cannot be said to give us knowledge, since Plato demands that all true knowledge is contact with what is truly real as opposed to mere opinion which deals with shadows, illusions, and copies of realities. In his *Philebus* he says that

> . . . the majority of the arts, as also those who are busied therewith, are . . . concerned with opinions and pursue their energetic studies in the realm of opinion . . . .
> (Ph, 59 a)

Consistent with this, Plato suggests in his *Ion* that it is *inspiration* and not reason which is at the source of art. The artist is seen here as the vessel of

the Muse which pours the beauty in.   Art is
inspiration, not knowledge.

Plato's Ethics and Psychology: Art can be harmful to the psyche

Since art has its source outside of the realm of
reason, Plato argues for a need to be discriminating.
In particular, a just society would have to be on guard
against art which distorts the truth, or in other ways
brings about potential harm especially to the young
who, as Plato says

> [A]re not able to distinguish what is and what is
> not allegory, but whatever opinions are taken
> into the mind at that age are wont to prove
> indelible and unalterable.   For which reason,
> maybe, we should do our utmost that the first
> stories that they hear should be so composed as
> to bring the fairest lessons of virtue to their ears.
> (R, 378 d-e)

Plato goes on to specifically protest against
those "poets and writers of prose" who

> speak wrongly about men in matters of greatest
> moment, saying that there are many examples of
> men who, though unjust, are happy, and of just
> men who are wretched, and that there is profit
> in injustice if it be concealed, and that justice is
> the other man's good and your own loss, and I
> presume we shall forbid them to say this sort of
> thing and command them to sing and fable the
> opposite.   (R, 392 b)

He also refers to the great literature from Homer, the *Iliad* and the *Odyssey*, which from his point of view sometimes tell untrue tales (that the gods, for example, are the source of evil and bicker among themselves), and can often inspire non-virtuous emotions like fear and cowardice.

For Plato, then, artistic values must be subordinated to social and moral values. It is Plato's view that the arts are to be used for the sake of the psychological health of the individual and community. In his *Protagoras* he suggests that the arts should help to build civic virtue in each individual, and

> . . . *qualities of respect for others and a sense of justice, so as to bring order to our cities and create a bond of friendship and unity.*
> (Pr, 322 c)

In keeping with Plato's psychology, the rational part should lead the others, especially the emotional part. The arts, as mentioned above, can too often stimulate the emotions. And Plato was concerned that the artist often

> . . . *stimulates and fosters this element in the soul, and by strengthening it tends to destroy the rational part. . . . For it waters and fosters those feelings when what we ought to do is dry them up, and it establishes them as rulers when they ought to be ruled . . . .* (R, 605 b, 606 d)

For metaphysical, epistemological, ethical and psychological reasons, a just society, according to Plato, needs to control the arts within it and must have discriminating tastes regarding those which are allowed and those which will be censored. Plato's is

no attempt to keep the arts out altogether. As seen
above, he is greatly aware of the ability the arts have
to contribute to healthy individuals and society.
Indeed, Plato himself has been placed by many among
the ranks of the great artists. His writings, including
the many tales and myths, are, after all, wonderful
examples of world-class artistic literature. And Plato
himself recognizes in his *Phaedo* that "philosophy is
the greatest of the arts." Art, nonetheless, needs to be
controlled if it is to have healthy effects. And, in my
view, there can be no better reason for Plato than the
role art played in the trial and death of Socrates. This
is a too often ignored part, I believe, of Plato's overall
concern about art. I am speaking here about the role
played by *The Clouds*, a play written by the great
Aristophanes which he very loosely based on
Socrates. Socrates specifically mentions the play at
his trial defense as recorded for us in Plato's *Apology*.
This play, Socrates attempts to point out, is really not
meant to be taken literally, because it distorts his life
and teachings. Aristophanes gives us a Socrates who
is a sophist (the sophists held ideas which Socrates
rejected such as relativism and skepticism), and who
busies himself with speculations concerning the
physical world (yet, as we have seen, it was Socrates
who shifted the focus from this area to questions
concerning the nature of the soul). It was a work of
art, therefore, which contributed to a twisted and
distorted view of Socrates. We can well imagine Plato,
who was present at the trial, realizing through this
example that the arts can have dangerous effects,
even if they are unintended, for Aristophanes' play, no
doubt, was meant as pure parody. The play was
rather like an ancient version of "Saturday Night Live"
media. Today, most people are sophisticated enough
not to take the images presented there (e.g., comedic
parodies of George Bush, Dan Quayle, or Bill Clinton)
literally.

Criticism and Analysis

It is important that we not repeat the mistake of those who overly generalize Plato's concerns with art and would have us believe that he chases all artists out of the just State. Fairness requires that we note Plato's recognition of the profoundly important and healthy role the arts can and should play in any just world. He was concerned only with that art which can distort the truth, play on the emotions, and provide a threat to the harmony of the state and of individuals, especially the very young. On the other hand, legitimate concerns can be raised about any society which attempts to control the arts. There are real questions about what in fact should be censored and who will make those decisions.

More specifically, however, we can ask some serious questions about Plato's metaphysical and epistemological reasons for controlling art. This can be done in at least two ways. One approach would be to reject Plato's views concerning the Forms presented as the only truly realities. This physical world of nature need not, then, be seen as some imperfect copy of that more real world. We could deny, therefore, that the arts—in particular the so-called imitative arts—deal in unrealities and illusions. If one holds that the earthly realm is also in some sense real (this is the position which Aristotle will argue), then art can be said to bring us in touch with reality and, consequently, knowledge. Another approach would be to accept, in large part, the Platonic metaphysics and epistemology yet believe that the arts do in fact get at the Forms, Ideas, or essences of things. One could begin, by arguing that Plato was too focused on realism as expressed in the visual arts, painting and sculpture, for example. In our own century, the arts have developed differing styles and objectives. The impressionists and cubists, for example, sometimes contend that they do at least symbolize the essences of realities. If the arts can in some sense bring us to the heart of reality, as it were, then Plato's objections in these areas could be overcome.

The question remains whether Plato's ethical and psychological concerns are well-founded. In the first place, there are many who are equally concerned about the effects of some forms of art on society and especially on the young. Such concerns have led the major television networks, for example, to utilize such things as advisory codes in response to a backlash from the public concerning too much sexual and violent content. Most people would agree with the need for some regulations on controversial art (the photographic art of Robert Maplethorp often comes to mind, or Andre Serrano's "Piss Christ,"—certain examples from Rap artists, too, such as Ice T's "Cop Killer,"or the genre of "Ganster Rap" as a whole can serve as examples here). If Plato is right about the young, i.e., that they are very vulnerable to information which becomes almost indelibly and unalterably fixed in their minds, then perhaps we all should be somewhat Platonic.

But real questions can be raised pertaining to Plato's contention that the arts should be controlled because they often appeal to the emotions. He seems to take this as an almost certain evil. But is it always dangerous and psychologically unhealthy to be so in touch with our emotions? Can human beings (as opposed to Vulcans like Star Trek's Mr. Spok) live healthy lives which are totally removed from the emotions? We shall soon see Aristotle raising these very points.

Plato does seem to be on the extreme side of this issue. For instance, he calls for the censorship of tragedies which focus on the emotions of fear and cowardice:

> [W]e shall request Homer and the other poets not to portray Achilles, the son of a goddess, as 'lying now on his side, and then back on his back, and again on his face,' and then rising up and 'drifting distraught on the shore of the waste harvested ocean,' nor as clutching with both hands the sooty dust and strewing it over his head, nor as weeping and lamenting in the measure and manner attributed to him by the poet Priam, near kinsman of the gods, making supplication and rolling in the dung, 'calling aloud unto each, by name to each appealing.' (R, 388 a-b)

One could easily argue that it could be much more dangerous and unhealthy to deny these emotions in and to human beings (even the idolized and almost godlike). Among other things, it may set up false ideals and unrealistic goals which are most often totally unreachable. And it is a puzzle why Plato seems so confining here. After all, he does recognize that all three elements of the psyche are important (the rational and nonrational) and are in need of harmonizing rather than abolition.

In the end, we must remember that Plato was himself deeply moved by the arts and specifically by the works of Homer whom he calls the "most poetic of the poetics" yet still he felt the need to *speak out . . . though a certain love and reverence for Homer that has possessed me from a boy would stay me from speaking. For he appears to have been the first teacher and beginner of all these beauties of tragedy. Yet at the same time we must not honor a man above the truth . . . . (R, 595 c)*

Selected Bibliography for Chapter Three

Copleston, Frederick, S.J.: *A History of Philosophy: vol. 1, Greece and Rome, part 2.* Image Books, New York, 1962.

Davis, Philip J. and Hersh, Reuben: *The Mathematical Experience.* Houghton Mifflin, Boston, 1981. Abbreviated (TME)

Guthrie, W.K.C.: *The Greek Philosophers: From Thales to Aristotle.* Harper Torchbooks, New York, 1960.

Hamilton, Edith and Cairns, Huntington, editors: *The Collected Dialogues of Plato.* Princeton University Press, Princeton, New Jersey, (seventh printing)1973. Abbreviations used: *Republic* (R), *Philebus* (Ph), *Protagoras* (Pr).

Sagan, Carl: *The Dragons of Eden.* Random House, New York, 1977.

Taylor, A.E.: *Plato: The Man and his Work.* Methuen and Co., London, 1949.

Tolstoy, Leo: *What is Art?*, tr. Aylmer Maude. Oxford University Press, 1930.

Vogelin, Eric: *Plato and Aristotle.* Louisiana State University Press, Baton Rouge, 1957.

Chapter 4

Aristotle:
The Arts and the Human
Person

Every man is either born a Platonist or an Aristotelian.
—Friedrich Schlegel

As we have seen, Aristotle (384-322 B.C.) was associated with Plato's Academy as a young man. Beginning around the age of seventeen, he continued his ties with that famous place of learning for some twenty years. Not long after Plato's death, Aristotle started his own school which he called *The Lyceum* and began to develop his own ideas, many of which take leave from Plato's theories. In the end, as Schlegel's quotation above typifies, Aristotle gives us a philosophy which in large measure can be viewed as a response to Plato's and which, as it were, provides the "other side" of things. In considering Aristotle's own remarks in his *Nicomachean Ethics* concerning his relationship to Plato's thinking, one cannot help but notice a similarity to Plato's own words concerning Homer:

> *We had perhaps better consider the universal good and discuss thoroughly what is meant by it, although such an inquiry is made an uphill one by the fact that the Forms have been introduced by friends of our own [Plato and the Platonists which followed]. Yet it would perhaps be thought to be the better, indeed to be our duty, for the sake of maintaining the truth even to destroy what touches us closely, especially as we are philosophers or lovers of wisdom; for, while both are dear, piety requires us to honor truth above our friends.* (NE, 1.6)

It is precisely because Aristotle offers a differing view in metaphysics and epistemology, that he is able to avoid many of Plato's concerns about the arts and the potential dangers thereof. Aristotle's life experiences, no doubt, played a role in these differences. To begin with, Aristotle's influences were different from Plato's in important ways. Plato, because of his aristocratic bloodlines, may have been bred for the political life. Aristotle was, on the other hand, the son of a physician to the court of King of Macedonia (partly through this relationship, Aristotle became tutor to King Phillip's young son Alexander the Great). Among other things, this gave Aristotle a sense of the complexity, importance, and reality of the physical world of nature and of the human body in particular. His was no Socratic-Platonic retreat, therefore, from *physis* to *psyche*. For Aristotle, the human person was more intimately connected with the world of nature than the Platonists had wanted to admit. *Psyche* is tied to *physis*. This accounts for the mature writings not only on the *Physics*, but *On Generation and Corruption*, *The History of Animals*, *On the Parts of Animals*, and *On the Generation of Animals*. These titles alone indicate that Aristotle was much more deeply committed than Plato to the importance of this physical world.

In conjunction with this we need to remember that for Plato, mathematics was the perfect model for how knowledge can be gained, principally because it offered us knowledge which was not tied to the physical world of change and illusion. Mathematics, for Plato, delivers us to the Forms, Ideas, and universal essences themselves—i.e., true realities. But the writings from Aristotle listed above suffice to show that for him the empirical sciences are also to be prized as models of true knowledge, and that the realities achieved there will be "true" realities. If we can be allowed to paraphrase and model a line after the dictum/prohibition over Plato's Academy ("Let no one ignorant of geometry enter here"), we can easily imagine a similar injunction over Aristotle's Lyceum—

"No one ignorant of biology may enter through these doors." Plato chided any attempt to gain knowledge from this sensory world of experience, Aristotle, on the other, begins his *Metaphysics* by saying that

> *All men by nature desire to know. An indication of this is the delight we take in our senses; for even apart from their usefulness they are loved for themselves; and above all others the sense of sight. . . . . The reason is that this, most of all the senses, makes us know and brings to light many differences between things.* (M, 1.1)

For Plato, all knowledge begins with the immaterial mind which is in possession of the Ideas and Forms which lie their, innately and in inchoate form, waiting to be brought forth by dialogue and reason. For Aristotle, knowledge begins with the senses which provide the mind with the experiences it needs. This overall difference between Plato and Aristotle is beautifully portrayed by the renaissance painter Raphael in his *The School of Athens*. At the center of this artwork (as sketched below) we find the older Plato (on the viewer's left) with his hand pointing to the heavens—thereby signaling that truth, beauty and goodness are to be obtained in that other, nonphysical world of the Forms. The younger Aristotle, standing next to Plato, thrusts his hand forward towards this physical world of our everyday experience.

Aristotle's View of the Arts and Their Impact on the Person

Given these differences with Plato, we can expect a contrasting position in the Aristotelian view of the arts and their overall impact on the human person as well. By way of direct comparison then, let us see just how Aristotle's ideas match up.

Aristotle's Metaphysics: Art can and does touch reality

Plato's concerns about art imitating a world (the physical world of nature) which was, in the first place, just a copy itself of the truly real world of the Forms, are discarded by Aristotle's metaphysics. In short, this physical world *is* the real world, not a mere copy of some other world. If art can bring us in touch with the world, then it can bring us in touch with reality. Furthermore, Aristotle has none of the Platonic disdain for imitation in general. He says, for example, in his *Poetics*, that

> *Imitation is natural to man from childhood, one of his advantages over the lower animals being this, that he is the most imitative creature in the world, and learns at first by imitation.* (Poe, 4)

Aristotle's Epistemology: Art can and does bring knowledge

We have already seen some of the major differences here. Unlike Plato, Aristotle is confident that knowledge is obtainable from our everyday experiences with this physical world. Therefore, since art can and does accurately reflect the world, it can often be a useful source in knowledge acquisition. But there is a deeper point to be made as well. Aristotle *does* agree with Plato that true knowledge lies in the form or universal essences of things. But

Aristotle offers us a view of "immanent form," that is to say, he viewed forms or universal essences as existing somehow *in* the very particular things themselves and not in some external, immaterial, Platonic world of the Forms. The human mind is able, that is, to abstract the common elements and universal patterns in things by its direct experience in the everyday world.

Given this view, the question remains, can art get at these universals or essences? Aristotle answers affirmatively. In his *Poetics* he says that

> . . . *poetry is something more philosophic and of graver importance than history, since its statements are of the nature rather of universals, whereas those of history are singulars.* (Poe, 9)

And again, in his *Metaphysics*, Aristotle says that

> . . . *experience is knowledge of individuals, art of universals, . . . [And] . . . knowledge and understanding belong to art rather than experience.* (M, 1.1)

Furthermore, keeping in mind Plato's attraction to mathematics because it seems to get at Forms better than any other science, Aristotle makes the point that the mathematical sciences are not unrelated to the chief object of art—i.e., beauty itself. In the *Metaphysics* he claims that

> *those who assert that the mathematical sciences say nothing of the beautiful or the good are in error. For these sciences say and prove a great*

deal about them . . . . The chief forms of beauty are order and symmetry and definiteness, which the mathematical sciences demonstrate in a special degree. (M, 13.3)

There is, therefore, at least some relationship between art and mathematics and in pointing this out Aristotle establishes another reason for being much more optimistic than Plato concerning the epistemological benefits the arts can provide.

Aristotle's Ethics and Psychology: The Emotions are not always a threat to the soul's harmony

We have seen that Aristotle objects to the separation between *psyche* and *physis* found in the Socratic-Platonic psychology. For him the human being is a unified creature where both soul and body are intimately connected. For Aristotle, psychology is tied to biology. We can easily understand, then, that Aristotle will see the mind's connections with the body, in particular the passions and emotions, as less threatening aspects. Aristotle's writings on this subject, as a matter of fact, have spawned much discussion and debate. I am referring to his ideas concerning one very positive effect that the emotions have on the soul, namely, their **cathartic** effect.

Aristotle discusses catharsis in only a few places. He promises a fuller treatment in the second book of his *Poetics*, but this portion of that work has been lost for centuries. We get a fair enough idea, however, from other references in the *Poetics*, concerning the potentially positive cathartic effects on the emotions:

> *A tragedy, then, is the imitation of an action that is serious . . . with incidents arousing pity and fear, wherewith to accomplish its catharsis of such emotions.*
> (Poe, 6)

Catharsis refers to a healthy purging of the emotions, either by purifying them, as it were, or at least by supplanting them as one can by allowing them an outlet in tragedy and other forms of artistic expression. Scholars usually offer one of two theories concerning what Aristotle really meant by catharsis. There are those, on the one hand, who see catharsis as a purification of the emotions of pity and fear themselves. This kind of purification is compared with that which occurs in religious ceremony. Still others argue that what Aristotle had more in mind was a kind of temporary abolition of the emotions. Here the comparison is with medicine rather than religion.

Plato was right, the arts can arouse the emotions like pity and fear. But Aristotle contends that it is wrong to consider this an absolute evil. The arts can help bring about a healthy integration of these emotions as well. Furthermore the arts have a variety of roles to play in society. In the case of music, for example, Aristotle tells us in his *Politics* that

music should be studied not for the sake of one, but of many benefits, that is to say, with a view to (1) education, (2) purgation . . . ; music may also serve (3) for intellectual enjoyment, for relaxation and for recreation after exertion. It is clear, therefore, that all the modes must be employed by us, but not all of them in the same manner. In education the most ethical modes are to be preferred, but in listening to the performances of others we may admit the modes of action and passion also. For feelings such as pity and fear, or, again, enthusiasm, exist very strongly in some souls, and have more or less influence over all. Some persons fall into a religious frenzy, whom we see as the result of the sacred melodies—when they have used the melodies that excite the soul to mystic frenzy— restored as though they had found healing and purgation. Those who are influenced by pity or fear, and every emotional nature, must have a like experience, and others in so far as each is susceptible to such emotions, and all are in a manner purged and their souls lightened and delighted. The purgative melodies likewise give an innocent pleasure to mankind.
(Pol, 8.7)

So the arts must be allowed to play various roles, not just the educative ones. Furthermore, the emotions aroused by the arts can have educative qualities by allowing for outlets or other forms of purgation. And in the end, there is a less serious "innocent pleasure" effect coming from the arts as well.

Criticism and Analysis

Because Aristotle offers different views in metaphysics and epistemology, and because he has a more positive outlook concerning the role that the emotions play, he presents a more optimistic picture of the arts and their effects on individuals and society as a whole.

But Aristotle's sanction of the arts, so to speak, is not without some conditions and limitations. In the end, Aristotle is in agreement, at least in part, with Plato's call for control. In the *Poetics*, for example, he says that there are several forms of plot to be avoided in the making of tragedy:

> *(1) A good man must not be seen passing from happiness to misery, or (2) a bad man from misery to happiness. The first situation is not fear-inspiring or piteous, but simply odious to us. The second is the most untragic that can be; it has no one of the requisites of Tragedy; it does not appeal either to the human feeling in us, or to our pity, or to our fears.* (Poe, 12)

These lines are very similar to Plato's objections to the poets and writers of prose who give examples of "men who, though unjust, are happy, and of just men who are wretched . . . ." The difference, however, is that Aristotle's objections are based on his view that in such cases the emotions of pity and fear will not be *rightly* appealed to. But Aristotle nonetheless agrees with some forms of control—he refers to the "censure" and the need to "condemn" the dance of "ignoble people" later in the *Poetics*, for example.

Finally, Aristotle's ideas on the arts are very modern and filled with common sense views. Concerning the role the arts play in the forming of society, he is again straightforward. In the *Politics* he says the arts provide "innocent pleasures" which are "in harmony with the perfect end of life." He continues there to say that the arts also provide relaxation and recreation which "also have some influence over the character and the soul," because "beyond question they inspire enthusiasm, and enthusiasm is an emotion of the ethical part of the soul."

Retrospective

Plato is my friend, Aristotle is my friend, but my greatest friend is truth.
                              —Sir Isaac Newton

We have seen some very real disagreements between Plato and Aristotle concerning the arts and their impact on the human person. But one central agreement between them is the view that artistic values are in some way subordinate to social and moral values (though Aristotle is less zealous in this area than Plato). By contrast, there are those who suggest that the arts have an intrinsic role to play in society, and their own independent values are to be honored in and of themselves. An example of this view is the "Aesthetic Movement," which argued for an "art for art's sake" approach, championed in the nineteenth century, by such people as author Oscar Wilde (we will examine his *The Picture of Dorian Gray* in a later chapter), and philosopher George Santayana. The other, more Platonic, side of things has been represented by such thinkers as the Russian Novelist Leo Tolstoy, who argued that "the best works of art . . . transmit religious feelings urging towards the union and brotherhood of man."

Both Plato and Aristotle would have rejected the "Aesthetic Movement." But there are some real difficulties that any society will encounter when it attempts to establish controls. In the first place, how will a society protect itself against any abuse of such controls? How will it defend against the use of art as sheer propaganda? There are many artists who have protested against Marxist countries, for example, because of the social controls placed on art—art is seen, from the point of view of many Marxists, as an ideological tool for furthering the fight against bourgeois values. There are others equally concerned about the "religious right" or other "conservative" movements who may attempt to control any art which they perceive as somehow offensive or out of step with "Christian" values. Senator Jesse Helms, for example, has been the target of many artists who perceive his tactics to be an example of "religious totalitarianism."

On a more purely philosophical level, the debate concerning whether artistic values need to be subordinated to others like the ethical and social, may revolve around how one views the universals of Truth, Beauty, and Goodness. Are each of these independent? Do each have, therefore, equal footing and value? If so, one could claim that the arts, in getting at Beauty, have a life of their own. The "art for art's sake movement," then, could be defended. For Plato, this is not possible.   In the *Republic* he indicates that all of the universals collapse, as it were, into one Form which he calls "the Form of the Good." While it is not at all clear what Plato precisely meant by the Form of the Good (the scholar A.E. Taylor likens it to the Christian's God), it is clear enough that Plato is suggesting here some sort of hierarchical scheme. Beauty must, in Plato's eyes, answer to the Good.   Artistic values must be subordinated to the ethical.   Since   Aristotle's   metaphysics   and epistemology do not give us any notion of Forms existing in and of themselves in their own regions apart from matter, we cannot credit him with a similar hierarchy of Forms. We have seen, however, that he does subordinate the arts to ethics and to truth.

We have raised some of these issues earlier, i.e., the relationship between truth and beauty. There we considered Keats' lines from *"Ode on a Grecian Urn"*: "Beauty is truth, truth beauty,—that is all Ye know on earth, and all ye need to know." Taking this literally, one need not be so concerned about subordinating the arts to truth; for beauty and truth are one. But what about goodness? Do beauty and truth always collapse into it?   Do they do so independently?   Or must beauty always be first bathed in truth before it can become good? Art can always have its own truth, but will it have its own goodness?

In the end, Plato and Aristotle care most about what is good for the soul and character of each human being and the larger society as a whole. The overall question they have raised continues to evoke us all: Are the arts always good for us?

Selected Bibliography for Chapter Four

Copleston, Frederick, S.J.: *A History of Philosophy: vol. 1, Greece and Rome, part 2.* Image Books, New York, 1962.

Guthrie, W.K.C.: *The Greek Philosophers: From Thales to Aristotle.* Harper Torchbooks, New York, 1960.

McKeon, Richard: *The Basic Works of Aristotle.* Random House, New York, 1941. Abbreviations used: *Metaphysics* (M), *Ethics* (NE), *Poetics* (Poe), *Politics* (Pol).

Ross, W.D.: *Aristotle: A Complete Exposition of his Works and Thoughts.* Meridian Books, New York, 1959.

Vogelin, Eric: *Plato and Aristotle.* Louisiana State University Press, Baton Rouge, 1957.

Wilde, Oscar: *The Picture of Dorian Gray.* New American Library, New York, 1962.

Chapter 5

From Augustine and Aquinas, to Leonardo and Michelangelo: Coming out of the Aesthetic Dark Ages

Philosophers after Plato and Aristotle did continue an interest in the questions raised by the arts and aesthetics. Stoicism, a school of philosophy which began with Zeno (336-264 B.C.) and which continued to flourish in the Roman Empire with thinkers like Cicero (106-43 B.C.), and Epictetus (c. 50-130), had developed a theory of beauty which was linked to the principle of an orderly arrangement of parts. A beautiful life, therefore, was marked by order, and had the practical and moral benefit of helping to produce tranquillity in the soul, a major goal of Stoicism. The Epicureans (founded by Epicurus, 341-271 B.C.), in their pursuit of a pleasure-filled life (though they stressed the avoidance of pain and displeasure, and disapproved of a life of excess), had questions similar to Plato's, concerning the possible dangers of some forms of art (music, in particular, according to noted Skeptic and historian Sextus Empiricus, c. 200). And Plotinus (c. 204-270), the father of Neo-Platonism, did provide an elaborate theory of aesthetics in various essays on "Beauty." In these works he rejects the Stoic identification of beauty with symmetry and order (since things can be symmetrical yet not beautiful; a corpse, for example) and replaces it with the Platonic notion of participation in Ideal Form.

As we approach the Middle Ages, however, we enter what can be called, with some qualifications, a period of Dark Ages for aesthetics. Aesthetics was clearly not a prominent area of focus for the greatest philosophers of the Medieval period, namely Augustine (354-430) and Aquinas (1225-1274). This is easily understandable, at least in part, when one recognizes the major intellectual trends of this time. The primary goal was to gain knowledge of and about God and divine matters. Augustine and Aquinas, typical of their age, were first and foremost theologians using philosophy as a tool, i. .e., a "handmaiden" or "helpmate" in the search for this understanding. Philosophy, in the end, had primarily an ethical and religious purpose. A concern with aesthetics or the arts in general, therefore, could at the very least serve as a distraction from what is more important, and, what is worse, might even endanger the soul by preoccupation with things earthly rather than divine. Furthermore, most of the arts (poetry, literature, drama, painting, sculpture) had connections to paganism in Greece and Rome. This undoubtedly presented some concerns to the pursuit of Christian philosophy and theology.

This does not mean that Augustine and Aquinas were totally silent on aesthetic matters.

Indeed, they both provide some important insights, which we will now briefly summarize.

Augustine

Augustine speaks of aesthetic issues randomly in such works as his *Confessions*, where he offers a warning against too much preoccupation with earthly beauty, admitting to a former "love with beauty of a lower order [which] was dragging me down." But he also gives some ideas direct attention in his "On The Beautiful and Fitting," and "On Music." What emerges is a focus on beauty as tied to order and proportion, unity and equality. Like Plato (in fact, Augustine can quite accurately be called the father of Christian Platonism), Augustine's psychological theories center on the notion of the harmony, unity, and order of the disparate elements within the psyche/soul. A beautiful soul, for Augustine, exhibits order. Thus, aesthetics is tied to ethics, since it helps us to see what a soul *ought* to be. And aesthetics has at least a symbolic tie to theology, since the ultimate end of the human being, for Augustine, lies in a "beatific vision," wherein the soul is able to "look" upon God as the source of all truth, goodness, and beauty. And beauties found in this earthly realm, when experienced rightly (for Augustine, this required God's light and help, i.e., "Divine Illumination"), can serve as symbols for the divine Beauty. Music, in particular, became for Augustine, as art historian William Fleming suggests, "a reflection of the divine unity of God and man; and the classical lyre, because of its stretched strings on a wooden frame, was interpreted by St. Augustine as a symbol of the crucified flesh of Christ." (F, 173)

Augustine also points to an essential difference between Divine creativity and human art. God creates out of nothing (*ex nihilo*), because He is perfectly free and omnipotent. The human artist, on the other hand, cannot be like God (because he is not perfectly free, nor omnipotent)—man creates by first receiving something, i.e., beauty as an eternal form, which lies in waiting. This notion will be revisited in our discussion of Michelangelo, and will play a central role for us as we later examine the notions of creation as presented by the existentialists.

Aquinas

Aquinas, in such works as "On the Beautiful and the Good," and also in his great *Summa Theologica*, develops some important notions in aesthetics as well. The *Summa* itself was a masterful development in theological discourse. Indeed, many art historians have noticed a structural similarity between the *Summa* and the great Gothic cathedrals of the Middle Ages. Fleming explains the comparison in the following way:

> [The] Summa *was as intricately constructed as a Gothic cathedral and had to embrace the totality of a subject, systematically divided into propositions and subpropositions, with inclusions deduced from major and minor premises. Every logical syllogism was fitted exactly into place like each stone in a Gothic*

vault; and if one of the premises were disproved, the whole structure would fall like an arch without its keystone. Thomas Aquinas' Summa *mounts the heights of philosophical grandeur, just as the vaults of the cathedrals reached the summit of engineering skill. (F, 284)*

In his reflections on art, Aquinas associates beauty with a trinity of notions (Christian thought is deliberate in its attraction to Trinitarian ideas). These are *integrity* (beautiful objects must be well integrated), *harmony* (beauty requires due proportion), and *clarity* (ultimately referring to the clarity of light, which has always been a symbol of divine beauty).

Medieval Art as Compared with the Classical Period

During the Middle Ages the arts suffered major changes as compared with the Classical period. In the golden ages of Greece and Rome, for instance, the art of sculpture flourished. In particular, it was common to find sculptures of individual humans, usually Greek and Roman heroes, portrayed as gods in idealized human form. These statues reflected the human body in all of its three dimensional, materialistic glory. Classical art, in many ways, represented a tribute to the human body and form, never before seen anywhere else in the world. In the Medieval period, by contrast, sculpted human figures were subordinated to very modest positions, becoming mere adjuncts, as Fleming says, "to the architectural and liturgical forms of the church." They were nearly never positioned so that they could be viewed three-dimensionally (usually being placed against a wall). This evolved into a "flattening process as applied to the human figure" as noted by art historian John Ives Sewall. Sewall points to the Middle Ages as a time when there was no "no reverence for the human body . . . . As a vehicle for artistic communication the human body—that essential of all classical art—was necessarily made useless . . . ." (S, 226)

The anthropomorphism of the Classical period was replaced with a turn towards symbolism in the Middle Ages. The purpose of the arts, as with philosophy, became that of a helpmate to the understanding of God. And since God Himself had warned against the making of "graven images," and because God cannot be adequately represented in literal form (how can the Infinite Being be literally portrayed in any finite medium?), allegory and symbol became the only realizable end for the arts. Even when humans are represented in art during the Middle Ages, they lose their three-dimensional, fleshy and materialistic shapes. For Sewall, this reflects "Christian asceticism and the negation of classical beauty," and "a contempt for the world, for material things, and for the flesh." (S, 227)

The subject matter for the arts reflected the Christian themes dominant in the Middle Ages (Madonna and Child, the Crucifixion, etc.). Even the most massive artworks of this period—the great Christian Cathedrals themselves—adopted a T-shape or cruciform structure, in order to symbolize the cross of Christ.

The Renaissance Period

All of this changed with the end of the Medieval period and the coming of the Renaissance which roughly spanned the fifteenth through the early seventeenth centuries in Europe. Art historian Helen Gardner notes that just as "the Christian Middle Ages evolved out of the disintegration of the Roman empire, so did a new way of looking at the world emerge from what might be called the Medieval style of thought." (G, 405) And what was this "new way of looking at the world"? In fact, the Renaissance period is more of a return and rebirth (as the French word "renaissance" suggests), than something new. The return and rebirth, that is, of the Classical approach. In particular, the arts and philosophy were freed from their subordination to religion. Plato and Aristotle were now read for themselves (a feat made possible by the proliferation of texts during this period), and not as mere handmaidens to Christian theology. The artists began to look again at the human form, and at nature itself as an object of beauty and inspiration.

The Renaissance saw the confluence of so many trends and social and religious upheavals. New worlds were being discovered by Columbus, and modern science was developing, aided by the many discoveries and inventions (the barometer and telescope, for example) which were used by the greatest scientists and philosophers of the day, the greatest of all, perhaps, being Galileo (1564-1642). It was Galileo's work which raised serious questions concerning the relationship between science and religion. His observations and mathematical studies had proven Copernicus' (1473-1543) earlier conclusions correct; namely, the heliocentric (sun-centered) theory over the Church-supported geocentric (earth-centered) theory. Coming out of the Middle Ages, the Church supported the view that man must occupy the central place in God's configuration of the solar system. The heliocentric theory was condemned by the Church (and Galileo was forced to recant this view) because it seemed to threaten the centrality of the human being, as a being made in God's image. During this battle between science and religion, the Church was also confronting internal and external struggles which led to the tumultuous Protestant Reformation (led by such men as Martin Luther (1483-1546) in Germany).

But this time of great upheaval and instability was also a period of freshness and optimism. Erasmus (1466-1536) offered a renewed enthusiasm for the classics, and developed a new style of expression in literature. And Michel de Montaigne (1533-1592) encouraged open and free expression of ideas in a "humanism" which offered a fresh concentration on the art of being a human being. Humanism came to be one of the central ideas of the Renaissance. Indeed, as Fleming points out, the dominating ideas of this period "cluster around three concepts—classical humanism, scientific naturalism, and Renaissance individualism." (F, 360) Humanism also had some deeply Christian roots, in particular, through the life and ideas of St. Francis, as Gardner notes (G, 405). For St. Francis offered a theology which included the real, three-dimensional and animal beauties of nature itself. The scientific naturalism flourished under the circumstances and effects of scientists such as Galileo. And the individualism, no doubt, was best exemplified by the quintessential artists of the Renaissance period: Leonardo and Michelangelo.

Leonardo da Vinci (1452-1519)

is undoubtedly one of the most brilliant men who ever lived. It has been said that he is "the epitome of the artist-genius as well as of the 'universal man' . . . [and] has become a kind of wonder of the modern world, standing at the beginning of a new epoch like a prophet and a sage, mapping the routes that art and science would take." (T,476) The world has long been moved by his great works of art, but Leonardo's intellect stretched far beyond the aesthetic world, into the philosophical, mathematical and scientific realms. Indeed, Sewall goes so far to say that "in spite of his great influence upon European art, it is a mistake to think of him as an artist. . . . A more accurate and fairer view of this great man's career would make it necessary for us to describe him as a scientist and engineer." (S,571)

Leonardo reminds one of Aristotle. Both had almost indefatigable energy, interest, and expertise in

widespread areas.   Aristotle taught and wrote
treatises not only on philosophy, but on politics,
biology, psychology, astronomy, comedy, and poetry.
And Leonardo reached beyond the arts into the areas
of physics, engineering, optics, geology, botany,
anatomy, military weaponry, and even aerodynamics
(anticipating human flight and the parachute, for
instance).   Leonardo adopted the Aristotelian
approach towards learning, i.e., the empirical method.
Everywhere and in every field he utilized the
experimental point of view.   Within his massive
Notebooks we find him saying that "If we doubt the
certainty of everything that comes to us through the
senses, how much more should we doubt those things
that cannot be tested by the senses . . . ." (S,572) As
Sewall notes, some of his contemporaries thought
Leonardo ill-educated since he seems to have had
little formal education into the great thinkers of the
Classical and Medieval periods.   To this Leonardo
replied "Although I may not, like them, be able to
quote their authors, I rely on that which is much
greater and more worthy: on experience, the mistress
of their masters."   (S,572)   Leonardo, again like
Aristotle, was aware that the senses provide us with
the world not as it is in an absolute sense, but in
multifarious and changing images.   He knew,
therefore, that our thought must sometimes penetrate
through the illusions of appearance.   An example of
this is his rejection of the geocentric theory (which
seems to be supported by the senses, and was even
adopted by Aristotle himself).   Leonardo's acceptance
of the heliocentric view may have been influenced by
Copernicus   himself   (who   first   proposed   the
heliocentric theory), since he and Leonardo may have
met during visits to Northern Italy.   Leonardo knew,
as Sewall points out, a great deal about the science,

in particular "that the earth's orbit was an ellipse and that its axis was inclined to the plane of its revolution." (S,573)

Another comparison with Aristotle is worth mentioning. Both men rejected the Platonic world of the Forms. In our last chapter we explored Aristotle's rejection of Platonism and the many effects of that rejection, in particular, Aristotle's emphasis on this, particular, sensory world of change (as represented in Raphael's *School of Athens*). Gardner notes Leonardo's conflicts with Platonism (G, 477), as do other art historians such as Robert Wallace and H.W. Janson, who tell us that "Leonardo emphatically rejected Plato's 'doctrine of ideas,' in which the plain evidence of the senses is denied. . . . Such a concept was contrary to all of Leonardo's thinking; it outraged him. He was first, last and always an artist engrossed in observation of the physical world . . . ." (W, 103)

Given Leonardo's Aristotelianism, it is also worth noting an historical irony. We have seen that Raphael's *School of Athens* represents the opposing viewpoints of Aristotle and Plato. The irony lies in the fact that, apparently, Raphael used an idealized portrait of an aged Leonardo as his model for the Plato figure (see F, 394). Of course, art does not always mirror reality, and in this case at least, art very badly misses it. Leonardo's likeness would much more appropriately fit Aristotle's image, and, as we shall later explore, it is Michelangelo's image which is more fittingly compared with a representation of Plato.

Leonardo's empiricism shines through, in particular, when we look at his landscape studies. The Leonardo scholar Ludwig Heydenreich, credited

him with offering "the first true landscape in art."
(W,30)   Leonardo provides detailed portraits and
drawings of nature, sometimes alone, such as in his
Arno Landscape, but more often as backdrops, such
as in his *Mona Lisa* and *Madonna of the Rocks.* Yet,
as Wallace and Janson note, Leonardo never regarded
landscape simply as a "backdrop for studies of the
human figure. He saw man in his whole environment,
as an inextricable part of nature." (W,29) Except in
the Orient (where landscape studies abound for
centuries before Leonardo), the world had never seen
such attention paid to the details of nature, revealing
the keen powers of observation in the artist.
Leonardo's view of the human being as bound up with
nature is clearly a break from the Medieval
deprecation of the world of nature, and became an
inspiration for and a precursor to the Romanticism
which we shall discuss in our next chapter. And
Leonardo paid careful attention not only to nature
itself, but to the creatures of nature as well. One
need only observe his many horse studies, for
example, to sense the labor of love that Leonardo
expended.

When Leonardo represents the human being, he
offers, as Garner points out, "figures [which are]
robust and monumental, moving with a stately grace
reminiscent of the Phidian sculptures of the
Parthenon." (G, 478) Again, we see the break with
the Middle Ages which offered the human body as
nothing more than a flat, subordinate, symbolic
element.

Michelangelo Buonarroti (1475-1564)

was a man with a tortured psyche. He seems to have had an unhappy childhood. He was a small, unbecoming boy, and was subjected to beatings by schoolmates—one such skirmish resulted in a broken nose, something which marked him for the rest of his life. Robert Coughlan tells us that Michelangelo was "tense, neurotic, always restlessly searching for a deeper significance. Everything he created reveals an inner conflict, an unreconciled struggle." (C, 6) Sewall says that he "disliked and distrusted everybody. He could not get a block of marble out of the quarry without quarreling with the workmen, and he never found more than a handful of assistants whose presence in the shop he could abide." (S, 599)

Michelangelo's disagreeable personality led him to see the older, more accomplished Leonardo, as a rival rather than as a colleague. He had an unhealthy envy, resentment, and dislike for daVinci. According to Coughlan, one of the reasons (though it certainly is not entirely rational) for Michelangelo's distaste had to do with Leonardo's proclamation that painting is a far superior art form when compared with sculpting. Michelangelo seems to have taken this personally. He considered himself a sculptor first and foremost, and a painter only in a secondary sense. Even when he does paint (on the ceiling and walls of the Sistine Chapel, for instance), he leaves a work which reflects sculpted qualities—the flesh and clothing on human figures reveal the hard edges and polished look of marble. In his contract for the great Sistine Chapel work, he signed "Michelangelo the sculptor" to leave no uncertainty about his own preferences (F, 373). Michelangelo had other complaints. He questioned Leonardo's patriotism, and his attitude and motivations towards art—in particular, he felt that Leonardo was an unprincipled opportunist.

In the end, Michelangelo may simply have been jealous. Coughlan points out that "Leonardo was almost everything that Michelangelo was not." (C, 94) Leonardo was handsome, poised, charming, and self-assured. He was the one and only artist whose esteem exceeded Michelangelo's.

Despite the personal differences between these two great artists, which are more or less unimportant, there are real differences in their philosophies of art. We have discussed Leonardo's Aristotelian, empirical bent. Michelangelo, on the other hand, was a supporter of the Platonic view of things. In particular, Michelangelo held to the Neo-Platonic conception of art, namely, that the beauty represented by the sculpted or painted work of art is merely a reflection of and participation in Divine or Ideal Beauty which it copies or mimics (remember Plato's *mimesis*). According to this view, beauty found in the earthly realm is only a copy of that True and Ideal Beauty found in God alone. "Had my soul not been created Godlike," Michelangelo writes, "it would seek no more than outward beauty, the delight of the eyes. But since that fades so fast, my soul soars beyond, to the eternal form." (S, 605) His later writings continue this theme and, in words very reminiscent of Augustine, he says "I have let the vanities of the world rob me of the time I had for the contemplation of God." (S, 619)

Platonism was, according to Coughlan, "the primary influence in Michelangelo's thinking about the nature of the world and of man, and about his own proper role as a man, a citizen and an artist." (C, 91) Other art historians highlight Platonic elements and themes found in many of Michelangelo's most famous works. Fleming, for instance, regards the Sistine Chapel design in this light: "His space is divided into geometrical forms, such as the triangle, circle, and square, which were regarded in Plato's philosophy as the eternal forms that furnish clues to the true nature of the universe. Next is a three-way division into zones . . . . Symbolically these divisions correspond to the three Platonic stages—the world of matter, the world of becoming, and the world of being." (F, 383) Fleming also sees individual examples on the Sistine ceiling as Platonic representations (see F, 386 ff).

A more subtle Platonism abides in Michelangelo's view that the artist's creativity is, after all, a divine gift from God. Plato had held that the artist was inspired by the gods. Creativity is here seen as a gift. The artist is the receiver of beauty, even before he creates it. Indeed, the artist does not really create beauty, but is the one who has the ability to find it where it already exists. Michelangelo's acceptance of this Platonic explanation of creativity is nowhere better illustrated than in his famous statues known as the "Captives."

These unfinished works were originally intended for the tomb of Pope Julius II. They give the appearance of a beautiful form trying to escape from imprisonment in the marble blocks. Beauty awaits the artist who has the ability to release it from its tomb. The "captives", according to Coughlan, "offer a clear demonstration of how [Michelangelo] worked: he would advance through the marble in so many parallel planes, almost as though he were peeling off layer upon layer of superfluity in search of the figure he had already seen in his mind's eye lying locked inside." (C, 167)

This theory of creativity, prompted by Platonism and embraced by Michelangelo, shall become a key theme for us as we proceed through ideas in the Romantics (especially the British poets), and lead up to the existentialists (where it will be represented again in the ideas of Marcel). It is the view that creativity is a reciprocal affair of giving and receiving. The artist, according to this view, is never the sole creator, never the lone giver of beauty. The artist, rather, is the one who receives the gift of beauty. In short, the human artist does not resemble the Divine Creator, who, as Augustine taught, is a Creator *ex nihilo*. The human artist always creates by freeing up the beauty which already lies there in waiting.

It is important to stress that, in our quest after meaning, we must all be seen as "artists" in the wider sense of the term. We are called to be creators. And what we are called to create is the content and quality of our own lives. In this sense, we are literally called to create our very selves. It is this, our self, our very being, which lies waiting as an empty canvas.

Selected Bibliography for Chapter Five

Augustine: *Confessions*. Penguin Books, Baltimore, 1961.

Aquinas: *Basic Writings of Saint Thomas Aquinas*, ed. Anton C. Pegis. Random House, New York, 1945.

Coughlan, Robert: *The World of Michelangelo*. Time Incorporated, New York, 1966.

Fleming, William: *Arts and Ideas*. Holt, Rinehart, New York, 1963.

Gardner, Helen: *Art Through the Ages*, revised by Horst de la Croix and Richard G. Tansey. Harcourt, Brace, New York, 1975.

Sewall, John Ives: *A History of Western Art*. Holt, Rinehart, New York, 1961.

Wallace, Robert: *The World of Leonardo*, consulting editor H.W. Janson. Time Incorporated, New York, 1966.

Chapter 6

Rousseau and the Romantics: the Role of Feeling in the Arts

Jean Jacques Rousseau (1712-1778) was in many ways a stranger in his own land and time. He lived in France during the period known as the "Age of Reason" or "Enlightenment." The spirit of this age was characterized by some of its notable champions such as Voltaire and Diderot, major contributors to the *Encyclopédie* which served as the guidebook and bible for the enlightenment philosophers. In this work, the philosophers (who called themselves *philosophes*) touted the many successes of reason and science and argued, in fact, that "Reason is to the *philosophe* what grace is to the Christian." The Age of Reason, then, decribes the attitude following upon the heels of the Renaissance which itself was in direct response to much of the dogma and authoritarianism found in the Medieval period. From the point of view of the *philosophes*, reason and science were now meant to replace faith and religion. These thinkers were optimistic about the progress of civilization which, in their minds, was now made possible by the advances in reason and science. They were convinced that the future promises more progress and even salvation, at least in the social, political, and economic sense, if not in the religious.

From the beginning of his literary career, Rousseau showed himself to be clearly out of step with these claims. He had, in fact, very real suspicions about this optimism and the promise for the future brought by the advent of reason and science. Indeed, Rousseau's first major writing was the award-winning *Discourse on the Arts and Sciences* wherein he argues that science and reason have made men worse, not better! In this work, Rousseau claims that "our souls have been corrupted in proportion to the advancements of our sciences and arts towards perfection." His ideas were rejected by Voltaire and Diderot, and it was easy for them to attack the *Discourse* since, as Rousseau himself admits, it was riddled with historical inaccuracies and weak logic. In the opening pages, in fact, Rousseau anticipates the criticism:

> *Running counter to everything that men dare admire today, I can expect only universal blame. . . . But then my mind is made up; I do not care to please either the witty or the fashionable.*
> *. . . How can one dare blame the sciences before one of Europe's most learned Societies, praise ignorance in a famous Academy, and reconcile contempt for study with respect for the truly learned? I have seen these contradictions, and they have not rebuffed me. I am not abusing science . . . I am defending virtue before virtuous men.* (D, 33)

Later in his *Émile*, Rousseau is even more direct about the inconsistencies and paradoxes found in his works:

> *Common readers, pardon my paradoxes: they must be made when one thinks seriously; and, whatever you may say, I would rather be a man of paradoxes than a man of prejudices.* (E, 98)

Rousseau never abandoned his skepticism concerning the promises made by the Enlightenment thinkers. He persisted in his attack on the so-called "progress of civilization" touted by the spirit dominant in his own age. And criticism was mounting against Rousseau not only from the proud protectors of the Enlightenment, but from the religious authorities too, who frowned upon Rousseau's attacks on organized religion, particularly his statements that "Man is born good" and that "there is no original perversity in the human heart." These ideas ran counter to the religious conceptions of human depravity and the need for religious salvation. Ultimately, the religious authorities in Geneva condemned his writings as "impious, scandalous, bold, full of blasphemies and calumnies against religion," ordered his books to be burned, and demanded that secular authorities place him under arrest.

Rousseau did not respond well to these attacks. He seems to have become extremely paranoiac, and towards the end of his life he suspected even his closest friends (David Hume, for example) of plotting against him.

Today we can better understand Rousseau's criticisms of the advances in the sciences by making a distinction between science and "Scientism." Many writers in our century have made the difference clear. The existential philosopher and psychologist Karl Jaspers (1883-1969), for example, often warned of the dangers of becoming totally caught up in an "objectified" world. Human beings are, according to Jaspers, "subjective" beings as well—the subjective self (understood wholistically) is in constant danger of being divided up. And Gabriel Marcel (1889-1973), the existential philosopher we will be looking at in a later chapter, has warned against "technologies of degradation." Technology, in short, is not an unalloyed good, and does not, therefore, always lead to advancement and progress. One need only think of the technologies of nuclear destruction to understand such concerns. More recently, Neil Postman has treated of the dangers of Scientism in his book *Technopoly*. There he tells us that Scientism contains three interrelated ideas:

> *The first and indispensible idea is . . . that the methods of the natural sciences can be applied to the study of human behavior. . . . The second idea . . . is that social science generates specific principles which can be used to organize society on a rational and humane basis. . . . The third*

idea is that faith in science can serve as a comprehensive belief system that gives meaning to life, as well as a sense of well-being, morality, and even immortality. (T, 147)

It is this last idea which best represents the view of science rejected by Rousseau. Science is wonderful, awe-inspiring, and rich in application, but it cannot save us! It cannot make us more moral! It cannot make us better as human beings! Indeed, we are in danger of losing ourselves by way of giving up our individuality and uniqueness. This is especially the danger Rousseau finds in social technologies—i.e., technologies used as a tool by society. Society makes us conform, it restrains our freedoms and our authentic modes of behavior. Rousseau laments in the *Discourse* that this was already happening in his own day:

> *One no longer dares to appear as he is; . . . in this perpetual constraint, the men who form this herd called society . . . .* (D, 38)

In short, society forces us to wear the mask of *persona*. Thus we hide from others and from ourselves. Society or the State can be a dangerous thing. And later in the *Discourse* Rousseau anticipates Marxist concerns when he says that men are in peril of being evaluated

> *like herds of cattle . . . [being] worth no more to the State than the value of [their] domestic consumption.* (D, 51)

The critic, however, has the duty not just to tear down, but also to build up. In criticizing the Scientism of the Enlightenment period, Rousseau does not confine himself to nay-saying. If science and technology cannot save us, what can? In answering this question, Rousseau helps give birth to the *Romantic Movement*, for he suggests a return to nature and to what is most natural within us. The direction Rousseau suggests involves an inward turn, in the style of Socrates. But he calls us to the voices of *feeling* and *conscience*, rather than to the inner voice of reason.

A most telling paragraph occurs at the very end of the *Discourse*, wherein Rousseau makes this plea:

> *O Virtue! sublime science of simple souls, are so many difficulties and preparations needed to know you? Are not your principles engraved in all our hearts, and is it not enough in order to learn your laws to commune with oneself and listen to the voice of one's conscience in the silence of the passions?* (D, 64)

Rousseau's inward path is a call to an innate and, in his view, trustworthy source which exists in each and every individual human being. For Rousseau, the true and natural guide for us all is not to be found in the realm of ideas. The famed philosophers throughout the 16th, 17th and 18th centuries had all called us to that realm. The *Rationalists* (Descartes, Spinoza, Leibniz) and *Empiricists* (Locke, Berkeley, Hume) had both called us to the idea. Whether it be the idea formed by reason (rationalism) or by experience (empiricism), it was still the idea which was at the heart of their search. But before we have any ideas, Rousseau argued, we have feelings! And feelings are among those "first impulses of nature," which, he says in the *Émile*, are "always right." The human animal, says

Rousseau, is truly a *noble savage* "forced to live in a town." It is important that we not let the town suffocate the savage. It is nature itself which provides our life-blood.

Romanticism

"Romanticism," among other things, is a description of the styles, intentions, and attractions of literary artists such as Wordsworth, Byron, Keats, Shelly, Coleridge, and Blake. It stands for a wide variety of notions all having, as Ludwig Wittgenstein (1889-1951) would say, a "family resemblance." The roots of Romanticism are found in its principle of the "return to nature." Responding to centuries of art which had quite nearly abandoned and ignored nature, the Romantics strove to call our attention to the great external wonders of nature itself. Nature had, during the medieval centuries in Europe, been viewed as containing awesome and frightening aspects. The writings of John Locke (1632-1704) and Thomas Hobbes (1588-1679), too, did not advance our appreciation of nature. It was Hobbes, after all, who argued that in the true "state of nature," the "life of man is solitary, poor, nasty, brutish, and short." And the Puritan settlers in America, the younger contemporaries of Locke and Hume, had a difficult time understanding the Native Indian population, in part, due to their very different view of nature. To the Native American, nature was not something to be conquered, tamed, and divided up. Quite the contrary, the point was to live in harmony with, and in great reverence towards, nature. The Native culture, no doubt, had an equally difficult time understanding why the White man so feared nature; a fear which at least partially explains why between 1600 and 1900 half of all the forested land in the United States was cleared!

The Romantics sought to reverse the negative view of nature by appealing to the wondrous, the picturesque, and the beauty of the natural world. And the "return to nature," was not simply a call to the outside world; it beckoned us to the natural world within as well. This call held to the assumptions of "primitivism," which is the view that what is natural in us is also, therefore, earliest and best (recall Rousseau's point that there were feelings before there were ideas). Indeed, the Native American Indians, so misunderstood by the early settlers, were much idealized and even envied by Rousseau and other Romantics. This has connections to the belief in the natural goodness of the human heart, which led Rousseau to deny such teachings as the doctrine of original sin. And the idealization of the primitive also leads to the glorification of childhood—our earliest and most natural state. Rousseau's opening lines from his *Émile* come readily to mind in this connection: "Everything is good as it comes from the hands of the Creator; everything degenerates in the hands of man."

In bringing us to the natural world within our souls, the Romantics return us to the realm of Feelings and Emotions; to the house of Conscience rather than to the house of Reason. And in doing this they also call us to our own individuality as well. Our feelings are, after all, *our* feelings. And the attitude of the Romantics, following Rousseau's lead was, "if I am not better than others, at least I am different!" This cry for individuality, too, becomes a major theme for the great existential philosophers, some of whom we shall study in succeeding chapters.

Romantic Poetry

Let us now explore several of the great English Romantic poets and attempt to find therein some of the dominant themes we have briefly outlined above. It is common among literature scholars to date the birth of English Romanticism with the *Lyrical Ballads* (1798), first published anonymously by William Wordsworth and Samuel Taylor Coleridge. We shall begin, therefore, with these two great men of genius and inspiriation.

William Wordsworth (1770-1850)

This selection is from Wordsworth's "Lines Composed a Few Miles Above Tintern Abbey":

Five years have past; five summers, with the length
Of five long winters! and again I hear
These waters, rolling from their mountain-springs
With a soft inland murmur. —Once again
Do I behold these steep and lofty cliffs,
That on a wild secluded scene impress
Thoughts of more deep seclusion; and connect
The landscape with the quiet sky.

    .   .   .   .   .

        These beauteous forms,
Through a long absence, have not been to me
As is a landscape to a blind man's eye:
But oft, in lonely rooms, and 'mid the din
Of towns and cities, I have owed to them,
In hours of weariness, sensations sweet,

Felt in the blood, and felt along the heart;
And passing even into my purer mind,
With tranquil restoration: —feelings too
Of unremembered pleasure . . . .

.   .   .   .   .

To them I may have owed another gift,
Of aspect more sublime; that blessed mood,
In which the burthen of the mystery,
In which the heavy and the weary weight
Of all this unintelligible world,
Is lightened: —that serene and blessed mood,
In which the affections gently lead us on, —
Until, the breath of this corporeal frame
And even the motion of our human blood
Almost suspended, we are laid asleep
In body, and become a living soul:
While with an eye made quiet by the power
Of harmony, and the deep power of joy,
We see into the life of things.

.   .   .   .   .

. . . And so I dare to hope.
Though changed, no doubt, from what I was when
        first
I came among these hills; when like a roe
I bounded o'er the mountains, by the sides
Of the deep rivers, and the lonely streams,
Wherever Nature led: . . . . For nature then
. . . To me was all in all. —I cannot paint
What then I was. . . .

.   .   .   .   .

. . . That time is past,

. . . For I have learned
To look on nature, not as in the hour
Of thoughtless youth; but hearing oftentimes
The still, sad music of humanity,
. . . And I have felt
A presence that disturbs me with the joy
Of elevated thoughts; a sense sublime
Of something far more deeply interfused,
Whose dwelling is in the light of setting suns,
And the round ocean and the living air,
And the blue sky, and in the mind of man:
A motion and a spirit, that impels
All thinking things, and all objects of thought,
And rolls through all things. Therefore am I still
A lover of the meadows and the woods,
And mountains; and of all that we behold
From this green earth; of all the mighty world
Of eye, and ear, —both what they half create,
And what perceive; well pleased to recognize
In nature and the language of the sense
The anchor of my purest thoughts, the nurse,
The guide, the gaurdian of my heart, and soul
Of all my moral being. . . .
(N, 259-260)

Wordsworth has written that "No poem of mine was composed under circumstances more pleasant for me to remember . . . ." The poem is important in a number of ways. It gives us a hint of Wordworth's own view of creation, i.e., it is a reciprocal relation between what is given in nature itself (and, therefore, perceived) and what the artist contributes ("what they half create"). In the poem we are also shown directly Wordsworth's own love, indeed, reverence, of the nature that is without and within. These lines speak to an interconnectedness between nature and the perceiver, and even between nature and the divine.

Some have argued that it expresses the most perfect statement of pantheism (the identification of God with the forces of nature and the universe as a whole) ever written. The poem gives us a sense, too, why Shelly called Wordsworth the "Poet of Nature."

And Wordsworth had the same sense as Rousseau concerning the innate connection between nature and goodness. In particular, this is seen in his "The Old Cumberland Beggar" (lines 73 ff):

. . .'Tis Nature's law
That none, the meanest of created things,
Of forms created the most vile and brute,
The dullest or most obnoxious, should exist
Divorced from good—a spirit and pulse of good,
A life and soul, to every mode of being
Inseparably linked. . . . (N, 249)

All good poetry comes, according to Wordsworth, from "the spontaneous overflow of powerful feelings." And it is from nature that our own feelings come, as Wordsworth claims in his "The Prelude" (Book 13):

From Nature doth emotion come, and moods
Of calmness equally are Nature's gift:
This is her glory; these two attributes
Are sister horns that constitute her strength.
Hence Genius, born to thrive by interchange
Of peace and excitation, finds in her
His best and purest friend; from her receives
That energy by which he seeks the truth,
From her that happy stillness of the mind
Which fits him to receive it when unsought. (N, 298)

"The Prelude" (final version, Book 2, lines 258-261) also provides another important message (besides and in conjunction with "Tintern Abbey"), concerning Wordsworth's theory of creativity, since there he tells us that the human mind

Doth, like an Agent of the Great Mind,
Create, creator and receiver both,
Working but an alliance with the works
Which it beholds . . . . (NA, 227)

Here Wordsworth echos a theory of creation which is in agreement with Michelangelo's as discussed in our last chapter—the artist/creator is not acting alone as a sole giver; rather, the artist is a giver and a receiver of beauty. As we have already seen, this view of creativity shall become a central theme for us as we move into the chapters on the existentialist philosophers.

And echoing Rousseau's concerns about education, Wordsworth continues in this poem (Book 13, lines 168 ff):

. . . And—now convinced at heart
How little those formalities, to which
With overweening trust alone we give
The name of Education, have to do
With real feeling and just sense; how vain
A correspondence with the talking world
Proves to the most; and called to make good search
If man's estate, by doom of Nature yoked
With toil, be therefore yoked with ignorance;
If virtue be indeed so hard to rear, ... (N, 299)

Rousseau's spirit lives and breathes within these lines. In his *Confessions,* he attacked the formalism of educational techniques praticed in his boarding school where, he says, "we were to learn . . . all the insignificant trash that has obtained the name of education." And we have already seen him lament in the *Discourse* concerning virtue, ". . . are so many difficulties and preparations needed to know you?"

Samuel Taylor Coleridge (1772-1834)

The following is from Coleridge's "This Lime Tree Bower My Prison" (addressed to Charles Lamb). This poem was written during several hours when Coleridge was unable, due to a minor accident, to accompany his friends on a nature walk:

Well, they are gone, and here I must remain
This lime-tree bower my prison! I have lost
Beauties and feelings, such as would have been
Most sweet to my remembrance even when age
Has dimm'd mine eyes to blindness! They,
        meanwhile,
Friends, whom I never more may meet again,
On springy heath, along the hill-top edge,
Wander in gladness, and wind down, perchance,
To that still roaring dell, of which I told;
The roaring dell, o'erwooded, narrow, deep,
And only speckled by the mid-day sun;
Where its slim trunk the ash from rock to rock
Flings arching like a bridge;—that branchless
        ash,
Unsunn'd and damp, whose few poor yellow
        leaves,
Ne'er tremble in the gale, yet tremble still,
Fann'd by the water-fall! and there my friends
Behold the dark green file of long lank weeds,
That all at once (a most fantastic sight!)

Still nod and drip beneath the dripping edge
Of the blue clay-stone.

.   .   .   .   .

A delight
Comes sudden on my heart, and I am glad
As I myself were there! Nor in this bower,
This little lime-tree bower, have I not mark'd
Much that has sooth'd me. Pale beneath the
    blaze

.   .   .   .   .

. . . Henceforth I shall
    know
That Nature ne'er deserts the wise and pure;
No plot so narrow, be but Nature there,
No waste so vacant, but may well employ
Each faculty of sense, and keep the heart
Awake to Love and Beauty! and sometimes
'Tis well to be bereft of promis'd good,
That we may lift the soul, and contemplate
With lively joy the joys we cannot share. . . .
(N, 390-391)

    Coleridge's attitude towards nature is reminiscent of Wordsworth's. This is not suprising since the two had a remarkable friendship which helped to fuel the inspiration and genius of both poets. Yet Coleridge's representation of nature was unique, argue scholars, in that they are "warmed by personal happiness and shrouded in a mystic, faery beauty." And in the last stanza of the poem, we see the workings-together of nature and the senses. Also echoing Rousseau, Coleridge was aware of the unmistakable connection between the inner and the outer. The locus of this connection lies with the feelings themselves. "Deep thinking," said Coleridge, "is attainable only by a man of deep feeling . . . ." The heart, the conscience, the faculty of sense, all unite the human being to a universe that is alive and indwelled with spirit. Coleridge's view of nature was a conscious rejection of the philosophical and scientific view of nature as Machine or Mechanism. The major model being confronted here, was Sir Isaac Newton's view of the world which was based on the clockwork model. Nature is perceived in the Newtonian view, as a giant clockwork/mechanism, and God is given the role of Supreme Clockmaker. What philosophy and science need, said Coleridge, is "the substitution of life and intelligence [for] the philosophy of mechanism . . . ."

Percy Bysshe Shelley (1792-1822)

In his poem "Love's Philosophy," Shelley refers to the divine interconnectedness of nature as well as everything within nature:

The fountains mingle with the river,
And the rivers with the ocean;
The winds of heaven mix forever
With a sweet emotion;
Nothing in the world is single;
All things by a law divine
In one spirit meet and mingle.
Why not I with thine?

See the mountains kiss high heaven,
And the waves clasp one another;
No sister-flower would be forgiven
If it disdained its brother;

And the sunlight clasps the earth,
    And the moonbeams kiss the sea:
What are all these kisses worth,
    If thou kiss not me?
(N, 1059)

John Keats (1795-1821)

Keats once said that "if Poetry comes not as naturally as Leaves to a tree, it had better not come at all." In his own works he exhibited the natural genius which was tragically cut short by his untimely death at the age of 26. Shelley, in his poetic tribute to Keats entitled "Adonais," said that "his fate and fame shall be an echo and a light unto eternity."

We look first at an excerpt from one of his letters which makes reference to the relationship between truth and beauty. The lines are reminiscent of those from the last section of his "Ode on a Grecian Urn" ("Beauty is truth, truth beauty, ...") which we have encountered briefly in previous chapters. The following is taken from his letter to Benjamin Bailey:

I am certain of nothing but of the holiness of the Heart's affections and the truth of the Imagination—What the imagination seizes as Beauty must be truth . . . I have never yet been able to perceive how anything can be known for truth by consequitive reasoning . . . . — However it may be, O for a Life of Sensations rather than of Thoughts! (N, 1210)

These lines are consistent with Rousseau's call for a return to the passions and sensations; to the feelings and the conscience; in short, to the heart itself wherein are engraved, he said, the principles of Virtue. And in calling for a "Life of Sensations rather

than of Thoughts," Keats reverberates the major
theme of Rousseau's *Discourse*, i.e., it is not reason
and science which can save us as human beings, for
our existence is tied to the feelings. Indeed, Rousseau
has stated it succinctly and clearly, "to exist is to
feel."

We also find in Keat's poetry the Romantic
sensations and connections to nature. Consider the
following example taken from the beginning of his
"Endymion: A Poetic Romance":

A thing of beauty is a joy for ever:
Its loveliness increases; it will never
Pass into nothingness; but will still keep
A bower quiet for us, and a sleep
Full of sweet dreams, and health, and quiet breathing.
Therefore, on every morrow, are we wreathing
A flowery band to bind us to the earth,
Spite of despondence, of the inhuman dearth
Of noble natures, of the gloomy days,
Of all the unhealthy and o'er darkened ways
Made for our searching: yes, in spite of all,
Some shape of beauty moves away the pall
From our dark spirits. Such the sun, the moon,
Trees old, and young sprouting a shady boon
For simple sheep; and such are daffodils
With the green world they live in; and clear rills
That for themselves a cooling covert make
'Gainst the hot season; the mid forest brake,

.   .   .   .   .

Nor do we merely feel these essences
For one short hour; no, even as the trees
That whisper round a temple become soon
Dear as the temple's self, so does the moon,

The passion poesy, glories infinite
Haunt us till they become a cheering light
Unto our souls, and bound to us so fast,
That, whether they be shine, or gloom o'ercast,
They always must be with us, or we die.
(N, 1138)

With Keats we are informed, as by the rest of the Romantics, of the deep connection between the human soul and the soul of nature. What Rousseau attempts to show in his philosophy, is given life and breath in the great poetry of the British Romantics. They give more example concerning the major theme of this book; philosophy can learn great things from art. Indeed, what philosophy wishes to say is often better said in art.

In their art, the Romantics try to make us feel and experience, rather than look and see. They do not attempt to paint a picture for us to view. A picture is meant to be looked at—as if to advocate spectatorship. The Romantics do not wish us to look at, but rather to experience life as true participants. The Romantics pave the way for a new kind of philosophy—existentialism—which was born in the second half of the nineteenth century with Kierkegaard and Nietzsche, and continued to blossom in the 20th. In our next chapter we will continue to explore themes given birth by the Romantics; principally the advocation of participation over spectatorship, and of the individual struggling against life in a crowd. In existentialism we shall also recognize the justification of the realm of the feelings, the acceptance of freedom, and of taking off the masks we all hide behind.

Selected Bibliography for Chapter Six

Abrams, M.H., general editor.,: *The Norton Anthology of English Literature:* vol. 2, sixth edition. W.W. Norton and Company, New York, 1993. Abbreviated (NA)

Cooney, William: "Jean Jacques Rousseau," from *From Plato to Piaget.* University Press of America, New York, 1993.

Durant, Will and Ariel: *Rousseau and Revolution:* vol. 10 in *The Story of Civilization.* Simon and Schuster, New York, 1967.

Noyes, Russell: *English Romantic Poetry and Prose.* Oxford University Press, New York, 1956. Abbreviated (N).

Postman, Neil: *Technopoly: The Surrender of Culture to Technology.* Vintage Books, New York, 1993. Abbreviated (T).

Rousseau, Jean Jacques: *Émile.* Barron's Educational Series, New York, 1964. Abreviated (E).

Rousseau, Jean Jacques: *The First and Second Discourses.* St. Martin's Press, New York, 1964. Abbreviated (D).

Stumpf, Samuel Enoch: "Rousseau: A Romantic in the Age of Reason," from *Socrates to Sartre.* McGraw Hill, New York, 1993.

Chapter 7

Kierkegaard and Nietzsche: the Art of Creating the Individual

Søren Kierkegaard (1813-1855) and Friedrich Nietzsche (1844-1900) are two of the most important thinkers of the 19th century. Their ideas have had a profound and wide-ranging influence on contemporary thought. There are many points of disagreement between them; Kierkegaard's intense religiousness, for example, finds contrast in Nietzsche's radical atheism. But there lives are parallel in many ways, and their ideas intersect in key areas giving us the fundamental themes of one of the most enduring philosophies of our time— existentialism. Let us begin by surveying some of these key themes.

Truth, the Individual and the Crowd:

In his "Concerning The Dedication to The Individual," Kierkegaard informs us that "wherever there is a crowd there is untruth . . . ." Indeed, he specifically states that "a 'crowd' is the untruth." Here we find the same passion for the individual echoed in Rousseau and the Romantics. It is only the individual who can approach the truth, and only as an individual. For, as Kierkegaard says elsewhere, it is only the individual who truly exists, because "It is impossible to exist without passion," and truth requires passion to be understood. In Kierkegaard, truth is personified, i.e., there is a real sense in which truth can be said to desire to be understood by the individual. We have already seen a sense of this (Chapter One) from Kierkegaard's search for the "why" of his existence:

> *The thing is to find a truth which is true for me, to find the idea for which I can live and die. . . . What good would it do me if truth stood before me, cold and naked, not caring whether I recognized her or not, and producing in me a shudder of fear rather than a trusting devotion?* (K, 5)

Besides passion, the truth requires courage, and only an individual can exhibit courage. A crowd by definition is faceless. One's individuality, assuming it is there to begin with, will be lost in the ocean of faces. The key characteristic of a crowd is its anonymity which promotes cowardice rather than courage:

For every individual who flees for refuge into the crowd, and so flees in cowardice from being an individual . . . contributes his share of cowardliness to the cowardliness which we know as the 'crowd'. (S, 238)

The crowd is specifically that place where one can hide from responsibility. In a crowd, the point is never to stand out. To stand out is to be an individual, and it is precisely the truth which requires us to stand out. This is, in part, what Kierkegaard meant with his famous claim that "subjectivity is the truth." It is the individual who is truly an existing subject, and it is the truth which exists for the individual. And so, for Kierkegaard, "the communicator of truth can only be a single individual."

Nietzsche also emphasizes the existing individual. In his monumental *Thus Spoke Zarathustra*, Zarathustra represents the true individual (for Nietzsche, this is the "overman") and says "I love him whose soul is deep . . . [and] who has a free spirit and a free heart." He has come, we are told, "To lure many away from the herd." The individual wants to live and stand for something, and "Whoever is of the mob wants to live for nothing." Zarathustra also links the truth to the individual: "To be true—only a few are able!"

For Nietzsche, to be an individual is to be a master rather than a slave; a master that is, of one's own life. The mob member cannot be a master, for individuality is carried away by the sea of anonymity. The mob fears masters and creates slaves. Society, which can operate as a mob mechanism, often finds a way to keep people in herd-like activity. We have seen Rousseau offer the same warnings concerning the herd-like characteristics of society. From Nietzsche's viewpoint, there is, as he claims in his *The Gay Science*, ". . . the fear of everything individual. At bottom, . . . [Society fears] the danger of dangers: the individual."

But why fear individuality? In part because it is much easier to live in the herd. One takes very little risk in "going with the flow." Indeed, it is out of a desire to live a safe, secure, and comfortable life, that the crowd derives its attraction for so many. It takes no passion to live in this way, if it can be called living. For Nietzsche, on the other hand, true existence requires something more:

> . . . the secret of the greatest fruitfulness and the greatest enjoyment of existence is: to live dangerously! Build your cities under Vesuvius! Send your ships into uncharted seas! . . . Soon the age will be past when you could be satisfied to live like a shy deer, hidden in the woods! (PN, 97-98)

Freedom, Responsibility, and Participation:

In fleeing away from being an individual and moving towards the crowd, one attempts to hide from freedom, responsibility, and participation. For Kierkegaard, this is an essential element of any kind of crowd:

> *A crowd—not this crowd or that, the crowd now living or the crowd long deceased, a crowd of humble people or of superior people, of rich or of poor, &c.—a crowd in its very concept is the untruth, by reason of the fact that it renders the individual completely impenitent and irresponsible, or at least it weakens his sense of responsibility by reducing it to a fraction.* (S, 237)

To be an existing individual, on the other hand, requires the freedom and participation to stand out or to take a stand. Freedom and participation mark the great challenges which lie before us as human beings. Each of us faces the choice, the great "Either/Or" as Kierkegaard was apt to put it. The ability to freely choose to participate is the bright side of the human coin. It makes us distinctive as a species. But the opposite side of the coin—responsibility—is what makes the choice dreaded. Indeed, dread itself is an important category for Kierkegaard who says that "dread is the possibility of freedom." It is always dread and fear of change, and of standing up for change, that marks the free choices in life. Security (the opposite of dread) is found in numbers. The crowd offers itself as a place to throw off our responsibilities. But in throwing these away, we are forced also to throw away our freedoms—to give up what is most distinctive about us—to give up, that is, who we are and what we stand for.

For Nietzsche, as we have seen, the greatest choice to be made is between existing as a slave or as a master of our lives. The slave chooses to be a crowd member; the master chooses freedom and responsibility. The slave wishes to follow what Nietzsche, in his *The Will to Power,* calls the "social instinct (the herd)." In so doing, the attempt is to "get around the will, the willing of a goal, the risk of positing a goal for oneself; one wants to rid oneself of the responsibility . . . ." Later he states it clearly: "Basic principle: only individuals feel themselves responsible." The courageous individual, we are told, is he that can "bear the greatest responsibility and not collapse under it."

Kierkegaard's Three Stages

For Kierkegaard, the fundamental human situation is one of estrangement and alienation. We are aware, he believed, of the difference between what our lives are and what they could be. This awareness or recognition brings into play the notions of the existential self (my life as it is), versus the essential self (my life as I ought to live it). This sense of alienation is accompanied by a feeling of guilt and anxiety—of falling short, that is, of our essential selves. Indeed, Kierkegaard's extensive analyses into the whole area of guilt, anxiety, despair, dread, etc., are among the earliest attempts to seriously understand these feelings. Freud, and others who forged the science of psychology, picked up this investigation later on. And in our own century, psychologists like Carl Rogers and Abraham Maslow have examined the Kierkegaardian theme of alienation. In Rogers' case, for example, there is the recognition of the separation between our actual self and our ideal self. And in Abraham Maslow we encounter the notion of self-actualization as the highest human need.

In Kierkegaard's philosophy, movement from the existential to the essential self is really an attempt to regain or recover what was formally lost. This sense of loss or falling short, matches the notion in Judeo-Christian theology of humankind's fall from grace—i.e., sin. And for Kierkegaard, the essential self can only be recovered when the individual makes the proper choices. Human freedom, once again, emerges as the major theme. We are, he believed, constantly confronted with the either/or—we must choose. And our choices determine who we are. We create and recreate ourselves with the choices that we make in life. For Kierkegaard, there are really three types of choices, or three stages for us to choose from. Kierkegaard's analyses of these stages literally comprise volumes. Let us briefly examine each of these in their turn, looking for key themes and characteristics.

The Esthetic Stage

The esthetic stage (from the Greek aisthetes=pleasure-seeking sensibility) is that level which Kierkegaard claims to be the "cellar of life." The esthete is one who lives by whim and impulse, feeling and emotion. Kierkegaard chooses the literary and musical character of Don Juan the seducer, as the model of the esthete. Don Juan is totally absorbed and governed by one desire—to enjoy the pleasure-filled sensibilities. For this reason, the esthete never takes anything too seriously. Taking things seriously requires one to confront the important and challenging moments in one's life. It also requires that one act on these moments and take a stand. This, in turn, would require commitment to principles, moral standards and the like. But these get in the way of the esthete's attempt to experience the widest variety (sexual, culinary, intellectual, artistic, etc.) of sense pleasures.

This stage falls short. Such a life can never be a fulfilling and authentic existence for a human being. A meaningful existence requires that we move out of the cellar of life and seek higher levels. The feelings of alienation call upon the esthete to make a choice: either to remain in the cellar, or to seek a truer form of existence. In either case it is his choice, his either/or. Unfortunately, Kierkegaard predicted, most will not move to the next level. In his *The Sickness Unto Death* he tells us that:

> . . . *unfortunately this is the sorry and ludicrous condition of the majority of men, that in their own*

house they prefer to live in the cellar. (SUD, 176)

The Ethical Stage

The one existing on the ethical level is aware of the failures of the esthete. Impulse and emotion are not proper guides for the human being. One must take certain things seriously. The ethical man does take things very seriously. He is guided not by the feelings, but by rules and reason. Moral rules of life provide a rational way of organizing one's life and of taking things seriously. The esthete's goal is to experience sensual pleasure, the ethical man's goal is to obey the rules of life. The model used by Kierkegaard here is that of an honorable Judge who follows all the codes of life. Life for the ethical man is simply a matter of following the rules.

But such an existence also falls short. This results from an awareness that I cannot, on my own powers alone, obey all the rules of life. No man can be ethically self-sufficient. Even great men such as St. Paul, for example, were aware of this inability: ". . . for what I do is not what I want to do, but what I detest." Hence, the ethical stage results in another alienation. In particular the ethical man falls into a consciousness of guilt and is without the ability to remove it on his own. This is precisely what St. Paul warns of: ". . . no one will be declared righteous in [God's] sight by observing the law; rather, through the law we become conscious of sin."

Furthermore, Kierkegaard argues that it is very artificial to consider life as a matter of obeying rules.

He was repelled by the idea, for example, of so many
attempts to make life easier. The proposal that life is
simply a matter of following the right rules, is one of
these attempts. In our own day, we are riddled with
the so-called "self-help" books which offer the rules of
life and the secrets of success. With this kind of
philosophy in mind Kierkegaard tells us in his
Concluding Unscientific Postscript (with characteristic
wit and sarcasm) that he has chosen the role not of
making things easier, but of making life harder:

> . . . *suddenly this thought flashed through my
> head: 'You must do something; but since it will
> be impossible for you with your limited capacities
> to make anything easier than it has been made,
> you must undertake, with the same
> humanitarian enthusiasm that inspires the
> others, to make something harder.' . . . Out of
> love for mankind, and in desperation at my
> embarrassing position, seeing that I had
> accomplished nothing and was unable to make
> anything easier than it had been made, and with
> a true interest in those who make everything
> easy, I conceived it to be my task to create
> difficulties everywhere.* (K, 194)

Kierkegaard lashes out against the artificiality
of a life made simpler by following simple rules. Life
is neither simple, nor is it about rules. Jesus
proclaims in the Scripture that "the sabbath was
made for man, not man for the sabbath." The ethical
man has things backwards. We cannot succeed in
putting rules ahead of life. We must choose, rather,
to live, and let the rules serve us as they may or may
not.

So the ethical man, too, must choose. Either to stay in this stage, continuously seeking and failing to fulfill the moral law, or to move to a higher stage.

The Religious Stage

The highest stage of existence, according to Kierkegaard, requires us to recognize the failures of the other two. We can bridge the gap between our existential and essential selves. We can achieve fulfillment in a meaningful existence. But we must rely neither on the sensuousness of the esthete, nor on the rational rules of the ethical man. What is required is not impulse and emotion, not rules and reason, but a passionate inwardness—a mode of existence that Kierkegaard called "subjective". In short, what is needed is faith itself.

The model for this stage is Abraham, "the knight of faith," who threw himself into the arms of God (took the "leap of faith"). Abraham's faith and trust in God was absolute, so much so that he was willing to break the ethical law and give up his son Isaac as a sacrifice to God.

But Kierkegaard also speaks of Socrates as existing in this stage. In the *Postscript* he tells us that "Socrates [lived] with the entire passion of his inwardness." And that "Socrates was in the truth . . . in the highest sense in which this was possible within paganism." If Abraham's faith is our model, then, he adds, we need to recognize that "Socratic inwardness in existing is an analogue to faith . . . . Socrates' infinite merit is to have been an existing thinker, not a speculative philosopher who forgets what it means to exist." Locating Socrates within the religious stage runs counter to the habit of many who typically locate him in the ethical stage. This is due to the fact that Kierkegaard (under various pseudonyms), sometimes treats Socrates as simply a "teacher of ethics." But, as Walter Lowrie points out, Kierkegaard "believed he could discern in [Socrates] a tendency to transcend the purely ethical by an approach to religion, not only in the sense of a relation to the absolute but in an experience of suffering and guilt." (L, 307)

In the religious stage, one holds fast to an "objective uncertainty" (precisely the state which requires passionate inwardness and faith). The rules are not there to help us. We are challenged to leap, not to conclude. We are confronted with choice, not with security. In this stage, we are given the opportunity to be in the truth as "Socrates was in the truth." To be in the truth is to take hold of it personally; to become one with it. This is another part of the meaning of Kierkegaard's "truth is subjectivity." Truth is subjectivity for at least two reasons. First, it requires a subject (the existing individual) to recognize it, and it is only the individual—as a subject— who can find a truth which can be felt at a personal level. Secondly, the truth is a Subject (namely, God is the truth). And it is precisely the relationship between the two (subject and Subject) that the religious stage recognizes. The existing individual (the finite and temporal) and the essential truth (God as infinite and eternal) are finally in relationship. Here then, for Kierkegaard, is the solution to our feelings of alienation, sin and guilt. The religious stage offers the only solution—faith:

When Socrates believed that there was a God, he held fast to the objective uncertainty with the whole passion of his inwardness, and it is precisely in this contradiction and in this risk, that faith is rooted. (K, 219-220)

The art of creating the individual, for Kierkegaard, takes courage and risk. It requires passion and commitment. The true individual does not wait for objective certainty before he acts. And what he creates is the greatest kind of art. What he creates is himself.

Nietzsche's Two Forces:
Apollonian and Dionysian

We saw that for Kierkegaard, the basic fact facing the human situation is the awareness of estrangement and alienation resulting in guilt and despair. For Nietzsche, the fundamental fact is the "death of God." This phrase is no doubt the most often repeated of Nietzsche's. It may also be the most misunderstood. Nietzsche's phrase—"God is dead"— is not meant to be taken literally. Taken in this way, such a statement would be self-contradictory. If God exists, he could not possibly die, since by definition God is an eternal being. Nietzsche is a poet as much as a philosopher, and his statement is meant to be taken poetically or metaphorically. The statement refers to the decline of belief in God in Post-Enlightenment Europe. A decline, we should note, which was certainly being encouraged by Nietzsche, for whom God truly was dead.

The death of God also signals the death of all attempts to find some objective Truth (i.e., The Truth) existing "out there" for the human being to encounter. The truth, for Nietzsche, does not and cannot exist. The sooner we recognize this (in accepting the "death of God") the better. What he is rejecting is the Platonic philosophy, for example, which locates truth and reality in some objective realm, i.e., the Forms. He is also, of course, rejecting all attempts by religion to place truth and reality outside of the human sphere.

In particular, Nietzsche means to call our attention to the all important consequences of the death of God. In the past, he argues, all human values and meaning have rested on the foundation which God seemingly provided. Now that God is dead, what will happen to our values? Wherein shall we find our meaning?

Nietzsche was convinced that if we did not answer these questions, we could well face an age of unparalleled nihilism, i.e., a culture wherein nothing (*nihil*) is seen as valuable, and life is considered as senseless, futile, and deserving of destruction. He even warned of potential chaos within German society and the world, and of wars more vicious than ever before seen. In light of the great World Wars which came after Nietzsche, and of Germany's role in them, his concerns are almost prophetic, or at least interesting. Is there a way out of this potential nihilism? The religious answer, for Nietzsche, was a dead-end. Could there be another path?

For Nietzsche we are left alone to create our own reality and truth; our own meaning in our lives. He was keenly aware of our need for meaning. In *The Genealogy of Morals* he says that "man would sooner have the void for his purpose than be void of purpose . . . ." In this work he also exhibits, like Kierkegaard, a profound awareness of human alienation and lack of self knowledge:

> We knowers are unknown to ourselves, and for a good reason: how can we ever hope to find what we have never looked for. . . .
> [We ask] "Who are we really?" . . . . The sad truth is that we remain necessarily strangers to ourselves; the axiom, "Each man is farthest from himself," will hold for us to all eternity. Of ourselves we are not "knowers" . . . .
> (GM, 149)

Just as Kierkegaard had predicted that the majority of people would choose to "live in the cellar," so too, Nietzsche seems to be suggesting that most will not have the courage to ever really achieve self-knowledge. We continually wear the mask (remember Chapter One). Nietzsche's entire philosophy is an attempt to encourage people towards self-knowledge (remember Socrates' "know thyself"). And Sigmund Freud once said of Nietzsche that he had a "more penetrating knowledge of himself than any other man who had ever lived or was likely to live." Like Freud (indeed, a full half-century before him) Nietzsche was aware of how unhealthy it is for us to hide from ourselves. And like Rousseau he blames society, in large part, for causing us to repress our basic instincts towards self-knowledge.

But what, again, is the way out of nihilism and towards self-discovery? The alternative which appealed to Nietzsche was that offered through the Greek genius. It was the Greeks, particularly the writers of tragedy, who had learned to deal with the forces of destruction. The tragedy we currently face is that left by the death of God (where will our values come from?), and the forces of destruction being threatened are those coming from nihilism. In using the Greek genius as his model, Nietzsche offers the aesthetic or creative aspect of human nature as the alternative to the religious. The question seemed to him basically aesthetic in the first place, i.e., how can one create (as one creates a work of art) a meaningful life?

In the Greek genius, Nietzsche sought after the very meaning of art and creation itself. There he discovered that art owes its existence to two forces— the Apollonian and Dionysiac. In *The Birth of Tragedy* he says:

> *Much will be gained for aesthetics once we have succeeded in apprehending . . . that art owes its continuous evolution to the Apollonian-*

> *Dionysiac duality, even as the propagation of the species depends on the duality of the sexes, their constant conflicts and periodic acts of reconciliation. . . . [T]hose two art sponsoring deities, Apollo and Dionysus . . . [Those] two creative tendencies developed alongside one another, usually in fierce opposition, each by its taunts forcing the other to more energetic production . . . . (BT, 19)*

For Nietzsche, the Greek gods Apollo and Dionysus are used to represent the basic forces within human nature itself. The Dionysian element refers to the unrestrained and continuous force within life itself. It was Dionysus, after all, who was the god of wine and frenzy, of chaos and intoxication. The Apollonian force describes that side of our nature which attempts to control the Dionysian dynamic stream of life, giving it organization and individuation. Apollo was the god of light and reason. It is our Apollonian side which creates order out of the chaos. This is the epitome of the creative act itself. For Nietzsche, true order (cosmos) can only come out of chaos. Nietzsche's Zarathustra makes this provocative claim:

> *I say unto you: one must still have chaos in oneself to be able to give birth to a dancing star. I say unto you: you still have chaos in yourselves.* (PN, 129)

It is obvious that Nietzsche is suggesting the importance of both sides of our human nature. Neither one in itself is good or evil. The healthy human personality requires both. In Nietzsche's analyses about these forces within human nature, he lays the groundwork for, among others, Freud's Id, Ego and Superego. And like Freud, Nietzsche is teaching us that the healthy personality must be a balanced fusion (order/cosmos) between warring forces (chaos) within us.

It is apparent as well, that Nietzsche is drawing a profound analogy between humans and God. God was thought to be that being which created the cosmos (the Greeks used this word to describe the universe itself) out of chaos. But God is dead. It is left up to us, then, to create cosmos out of chaos. Indeed, we must replace God (The Creator) with ourselves (creators) and become artists—the most godlike of all beings. And just as Kierkegaard had his model (Socrates), so too, Nietzsche chooses the model of the great German poet Goethe. In the *Twilight of The Idols* he describes Goethe as:

> not a German event but a European one; a magnificent attempt to overcome . . . a kind of self-overcoming . . . . [H]e did not retire from life but put himself into the midst of it; he was not fainthearted but took as much as possible upon himself, over himself, into himself. What he wanted was totality; . . . he disciplined himself to wholeness, he created himself. (PN, 553-554)

Nietzsche coined the term "overman" (*übermensch*) to describe those who, like Goethe, have learned to overcome the tragedies of the human world. And, for Nietzsche, it is only by turning to the human world that we can overcome it and ourselves. We cannot seek for our meaning in some otherworldly way, since God is dead. And so we find these pivotal passages in *Zarathustra*:

Lead back to the earth the virtue that flew away, as I do
—back to the body, back to life, that it may give the earth a meaning, a human meaning.

> .   .   .   .   .

The human world, the human sea: that is where I now cast my golden fishing rod and say: Open up, you human abyss!

> .   .   .   .   .

You creators, you higher men! One is pregnant only with one's own child.
(PN, 188, 350, 402)

In the end, the tragedy of the death of God (where shall I find meaning and value in life?) is reversed. Nietzsche argues that if God did exist, my freedom would be lost. Zarathustra calls us away "from God and gods . . . . [For] what could one create if gods existed?" And in *The Gay Science* he writes that the consequences of the death of God,

> . . . *are perhaps the reverse of what one might expect: not all sad and dark, but rather like a new, scarcely describable kind of light, ... Indeed, we philosophers and 'free spirits' feel as if a new dawn were shining on us . . . At last the horizon appears free again to us, even granted that it is not bright; at last our ships may venture out again, venture out in the face of danger; all the danger of the lover of knowledge is permitted*

*again; the sea, our sea, lies open again; perhaps
there has never yet been such an 'open sea.'*
(PN, 447-448)

Retrospective

We have seen Kierkegaard and Nietzsche
agreeing on several important themes: we should
become true individuals and refuse to hide out in
crowds; we should embrace our freedom and, at the
same time, not shun the consequence of freedom—
responsibility.

There are other noteworthy comparisons as
well.   Kierkegaard's commitment to truth as
subjectivity, for example, finds some counterpart in
Nietzsche for whom truth is not an "objective" datum
"out there" for us to discover. Indeed, for Nietzsche,
the subjectivity of truth is perhaps even more radical
than in Kierkegaard. In his *The Genealogy of Morals*,
for example, Nietzsche tells us that "All seeing is
essentially perspective, and so is all knowing." In the
end, however, both thinkers agree upon and highlight
the personal (subjective) element in truth—they both
believe that each of us must make personal
investment into our truths.

There are, of course, major differences between
these two thinkers. We have seen in Kierkegaard, for
example, that the fundamental datum is the guilt we
experience at not being our essential selves. But for
Nietzsche, feelings of guilt are not necessarily
trustworthy reflections on the human condition. In

the *Genealogy* he says that "The fact that a person thinks himself 'guilty' or 'sinful' is no proof that he is so, any more than the fact that a person feels healthy is a proof of his health." Earlier in the same work he argues that "man's will to find himself guilty" is a form of "psychological cruelty" and "an insanity of the will that is without parallel."

The central difference between these two thinkers is found in the direction of their passionate interest. For the "passionate inwardness" in Kierkegaard is directed towards the very much alive God with whom the person has, in the leap of faith, a profound personal relationship. The passion in Nietzsche, on the other hand, is directed towards an absence; i.e., the death of God. Nowhere in Nietzsche, is this more passionately expressed than in the section of *The Gay Science* called "The Madman":

> *"Whither is God" he cried. "I shall tell you. We have killed him—you and I. All of us are his murderers. But how have we done this? How were we able to drink up the sea? Who gave us the sponge to wipe away the entire horizon? What did we do when we unchained this earth from its sun? Whither is it moving now? Whither are we moving now? Away from all suns? Are we not plunging continually? Backward, sideward, forward, in all directions? Is there any up or down left? Are we not straying as through an infinite nothing? Do we not feel the breath of empty space? . . . God is dead. God remains dead. And we have killed him. . . . Is not the greatness of this deed too great for us?*

Must not we ourselves become gods simply to seem worthy of it? . . ." (PN, 95-96)

For both of our thinkers, the key is to create ourselves as individuals. Yet, for Nietzsche, that creation seems to be a divine act indeed. It requires us to create *ex-nihilo* (out of nothing). To do this, we must become gods ourselves. Yet if the death of God brings a truly open sea and a horizonless world—where there is no more absolute up and down—then by what standard shall we measure our choices?

For both Kierkegaard and Nietzsche, as we have seen, it is choice which can bring us to a meaningful existence (for Kierkegaard, this is the religious stage; for Nietzsche, it is the overman and master). But if Nietzsche is right—God is dead—how can we consistently call the master's existence a "higher" form of existence than the slave's? Without any up and down, there does not seem to be any backdrop against which one could measure forms or levels of existence.

The real question here seems to be whether we can, indeed, become gods; whether we can, afterall, create as God creates, i.e., *ex nihilo*. We shall have to explore this question in our next chapter, as we examine the ideas of Gabriel Marcel and Jean Paul Sartre, two twentieth-century thinkers who were very much influenced by the thought of Kierkegaard and Nietzsche.

Selected Bibliography for Chapter Seven

Bretall, Robert: Editor, *A Kierkegaard Anthology*. Modern Library, New York, 1946. Abbreviated (K).

Kaufmann, Walter: Translator, *The Portable Nietzsche*. The Viking Press, New York, 1961. Abbreviated (PN).

Kierkegaard, Søren: *The Sickness Unto Death*, translated by Walter Lowrie. Princeton University Press, Princeton, NJ, 1974. Abbreviated (SUD).

——————: *Either/Or* volume I, translated by David F. Swenson. Anchor Books, New York, 1959. *Either/Or* volume II, translated by Walter Lowrie. Princeton University Press, Princeton, NJ, 1971.

Lowrie, Walter: *Kierkegaard*, volume two. Harper Torchbooks, New York, 1962. Abbreviated (L).

Nietzsche, Friedrich: *The Birth of Tragedy* and *The Genealogy of Morals*, translated by Francis Golffing. Doubleday, New York, 1956. Abbreviated as (BT) and (GM).

——————: *The Will to Power*, edited by Walter Kaufmann. Vintage Books, New York, 1968.

Spanos, William: *A Casebook on Existentialism.* Thomas Y. Crowell Co., New York, 1969. Abbreviated (S). Also in (S): "Concerning the Dedication to the Individual" (CDI).

Chapter 8

Marcel and Sartre: On the Nature of Creation, Human and Divine

Gabriel Marcel (1889-1973) and Jean-Paul Sartre (1905-1980) are important representatives of existentialism in the 20th century. Sartre accepted the label "existentialist," whereas Marcel preferred the title "Neo-Socratic." One way of distinguishing them is to suggest that Marcel carries on the tradition of religious existentialism begun by Kierkegaard, while Sartre continues the atheistic existentialism introduced by Nietzsche.

These two men held widely different views concerning the nature of the human person and, as we shall see, on the creative acts that persons are capable of. Let us begin by taking each thinker in their turn.

Marcel

Gabriel Marcel was born in Paris, France, the son of an educated man who held administrative positions in France's National Museum and Library, and also served as French ambassador to Stockholm. This no doubt influenced Marcel's cultured and studious character. His mother died when he was only four years old, and Marcel was later to write of the profound impact this had on him; it was completely sudden and shook the entire family. He was raised primarily by his aunt who was Jewish, but converted to Protestant Christianity. Her religious disposition served as a contrast to his father's more agnostic spirit (he was raised a Catholic but ceased to practice religion at an early age). Marcel himself converted to Catholicism later in his mature life (sometime in his forties). By this time, however, most of his philosophical ideas had already been developed.

As a young man during World War I, Marcel worked for the Red Cross. His job was to obtain information on deceased soldiers for their loved ones. Never satisfied with the information they received, the survivors always desired more answers than he was able to give. He began to experience the incompleteness of such answers—can anyone fully explain to parents why their son has died? Later he wrote that the effect of this experience "was to make me reflect upon the limitations of any inquiry or questionnaire, so that I began to ask myself if it was not possible to get beyond the sphere of question and answer." And in his mature thinking he began to ask the kind of questions which did not admit of ready-made solutions. Many of the issues he raised were either already or fast becoming the major themes of existentialism. We have already traced some of the major themes of this movement, in the previous chapter, to Kierkegaard and Nietzsche. As its name indicates, existentialism is primarily concerned with human existence, and it poses such issues as; what does it mean to be an existing subject? do I begin my existence with a blank slate (are all my future possibilities open and undetermined?), or is my nature or essence already in large part determined?, does life have some inherent or objective meaning, or is it up to me to provide that meaning subjectively? These questions along with many other and related issues form the foundation of existentialism. But what also distinguishes the existentialist is a particular kind of method or style of doing philosophy. Beginning with Kierkegaard, existentialism has always rejected the system-building approach in philosophy. The issues that they raise, they argue, cannot be addressed in the normal fashion of deriving conclusions from previous premises and then stacking them all together like so many building blocks. Rather, the issues must be approached on the level of existence, i.e., as a lived experience. This means that as an existing subject one must not approach existential questions in a purely objective manner. They must be experienced if one is to have any hope of really understanding them.

This may explain why most existentialists pursue alternative routes to the traditional treatise. Many have written plays and novels—indeed, Jean Paul Sartre and Albert Camus have received the Nobel Prize in literature. Marcel is no exception to this, contributing plays and journals. In fact, he made much of his living as an art critic. For Marcel, the method of preference is one which sees itself akin to an "exploration or digging." The questions raised by the philosopher are really an invitation to a journey, and the human person is defined by Marcel as a *homo viator*, a wayfarer, a traveler. The journey, too, is a "winding path" with no real end in sight.

This commitment on behalf of the existentialists does tend to make our reading of them a little more difficult. They choose not to be deductive and systematic in their approach. In Marcel's case, however, we are left with certain pairs of ideas which provide guidance.

Problem vs. Mystery

The first pair or distinction is that between problem and mystery. This is really an epistemological distinction having to do with two ways in which we can attempt to gain knowledge. A problem describes an object or thing set before me as an obstacle in my path requirinq a solution. Another aspect of any problem is that it is anonymous in nature. That is to say, the problem does not require any specific person to solve it. It is there waiting for anyone at all and no one in particular; i.e., anyone with the requisite abilities will do. This points up the feature of externality as well. A problem is external or outside of me or anyone in particular; it exists in its own realm apart from any person or persons. One can think, for example, of a math problem which vexes us, or a problem with that "damned" machine over there that I cannot fix! Many things are problems, and need to be approached as such. In fact, in large part, science is that discipline which deals with problems, and it is necessary and important to recognize how crucial problem solving is. But it is even more important, says Marcel, that we understand that not everything can be treated on this level. There are certain fundamental questions which do not fit the model of a problem. As an example, he cites the questions asked by the existentialist as indicated above. The example he often uses is the question "who am I?". Such a question does not indicate that the questioner is suffering from amnesia. Marcel is interested in such a question when it is asked on the more fundamental level; who or what am I?, where did I come from anyway?, where am I going?, how much control do I have over my own destiny?, is there a God in control of it all? Such questions cannot be handled as problems. We are not dealing with an issue set before us as an obstacle out there and external to us, for we are the issue at hand. Nor are these issues anonymous. Rather, they are intensely personal questions which do involve us, and specifically us, not just anyone in general. Nor, thinks Marcel, do such questions give way to ultimate solutions. Problems have solutions, but these questions lead us to the winding path. Each one opens a door to new and equally non-problematical questions. All such questions are called "mysteries." In some cases, Marcel chooses the term "metaproblematical" to signal that mysteries literally take us beyond the realm of problem (*meta* = "beyond" in Greek).   Finally, the attitude on the level of problems is that of curiosity.   Marcel distinguishes this from what he calls "metaphysical uneasiness"— the attitude taken up on the level of mystery. I am curious to see, for example, the solution to this or that problem—a math problem, or the machine requiring fixing. But on the level of mystery—who am I?—I have moved beyond mere curiosity. I approach such issues with a heightened interest (think of the Latin *inter esse*—it involves my very being; it signals something I am concerned with and about), wonder, or awe. In profound cases, I approach with a certain uneasiness in being (metaphysical uneasiness).

Spectator vs. Participant

Another major distinction evolves from an understanding of the differences between problems and mysteries.   This is the distinction between spectator and participant. With this pair, Marcel is describing different ways one can relate to the world, to others, or to oneself. The spectator sees himself as external to what he is looking at. All things, including other people and himself, become problems to be solved. He desires only to see the solution, to figure out the answer. This is acceptable on the level of problems, but fails on the level of mystery. In doing so, warns Marcel, the spectator isolates himself from all real contact with what it is he seeks to understand. The world of the spectator is the ego-centric world. From the spectator's point of view, everything else in the world revolves around him. He is clearly the center of his world. But the spectator becomes alienated in this process.   Some things are not spectacles to be observed from afar. Some things (for example, relationships with others) demand personal involvement and interaction. The participant realizes that his participation is required if he is to make any progress. The world, the real world, is the one that I live in and experience. The world of the spectator is ultimately an unreal fiction; a poor copy at best, just as pictures are only facsimiles of what they represent. In the end, the participant realizes that life is not a show to be watched, but an experience to be lived.

Having vs. Being

This pair also becomes interwoven with the previous distinctions. The spectator—the one who deals with the world as if it were a problem to be solved—desires in the end to *have* or *possess* it in so far as he can. He seeks the solution so that he can manipulate reality to suit his own purposes. Here the true picture of the spectator emerges; he sees all things, even other human beings, as objects to be figured out so that they can be controlled. An immediate image that comes to mind is the aspiring corporate executive who sees all other employees as pawns on the chessboard to be conquered, or as steps on his ladder of "success." The participant, on the other hand, does *not* desire *to have, but to be.* He understands that some things, especially other persons, are not there for me to possess. Instead they offer me the possibility of involvement, interchange, and reciprocity. *I, as participant, desire to be a person, not to have persons.* Consider the one who defines others according to what they have or possess; "he owns a Porsche, and is therefore worthy of my attention." This involves a fundamental ignoring of the *important difference between who I am and what I have.* Marcel once said that in America a man can be worth a million dollars even if as a man he is worth nothing.   With this, Marcel seems to point out America (though not in an exclusive sense) as the country which values possessions above all else. The millionaire is the achiever. The millionaire embodies success.   It does not seem to matter very much whether the millionaire is worthwhile as a person. He may be a success at big business and return home only to abuse his wife and kids, but he is still a "success."

Marcel is suggesting that we need to break the habit of having, and turn towards being. Ultimately, the haver loses not only contact with others but also with himself. It is an ironic but recognizable truth that the possessor ends up being the possessed. The haver becomes had. For Marcel, this is because the human person needs real being-level contact with other human beings. The solitary self is isolated from others and suffers a "sclerosis" which hardens around him. The way out requires an opening up. The haver is not open to others, the very essence of his being is "closed."   Having is finally transcended, teaches Marcel, only in being-relationships like love and fidelity. And love and fidelity, for Marcel, are above all creative acts (One of his major works was entitled *Creative Fidelity*).   We turn next, therefore, to a discussion of Marcel's views concerning creativity.

Marcel on Creation

Creation occurs at the level of mystery

In his book *Being and Having*, Marcel says that the traditional distinction between knower and thing known, doer and thing done, etc., namely, that distinction which characterizes the level of problems, "breaks down" whenever we are in the realm of artistic creation. In musical creation, for example, he says that we are "in a sphere where the thing stated cannot be distinguished from the manner of stating it." In addition, in *Tragic Wisdom and Beyond* he argues that creation (in art and poetry, for example) "rests on a foundation of personal involvement . . . a personal response to a call." Furthermore, in his *Searchings*, Marcel suggests a connection between dramatic creation and a "restless heart." Remember that one who works on the level of problems, for Marcel, carries the attitude of curiosity, not the metaphysical uneasiness and wonder which is needed on the level of mystery. Clearly, then, Marcel offers a view of creativity as occurring in the realm of mystery rather than problems.

Creation rejects spectatorship and requires participation

In an early work entitled *Philosophical Fragments*, Marcel says that "wherever there is creation . . . there is participation." And in his *The Mystery of Being*, part one, he argues that the artist (by way of example, he is speaking of Vermeer) could never be "reduced to the condition of a mere spectator." In part two of the same work we learn that "dramatic creation, where the creation is authentic, consists in the exorcising of the ego-centric spirit." And we have seen that the ego-centric viewpoint is that which is adopted and maintained by the spectator. We learn more about this from Marcel's *The Philosophy of Existence*, where he argues that "artistic creation . . . excludes the act of self-centering . . . ."

In the end, Marcel teaches us that the reason creation is impossible within the point of view of spectatorship, is because the spectator closes himself off from authentic reception. We will learn more about this later.

Creativity escapes having and reaches being

In *Man Against Mass Society*, Marcel tells us that "being creative is related to being open towards others . . . ." And it is precisely the haver who is not open to others. In *Being and Having* he says that creation is the "liberation of what cannot be shown." And it is the realm of having wherein the desire to possess and to show my possessions festers and destroys. He goes on to explain that "As soon as there is creation, in whatever degree, we are in the realm of being . . . ." And that "The more creation can shake [having] off, the nearer it is to absolute creation."

Clearly then, creation has its source and its conclusion in the realm of being. And as long as one remains in the mode of having, true creation is not possible.

Sartre

Jean Paul Sartre was born into a celebrated Swiss-French family which included his renowned cousin Albert Schweitzer, the world famous missionary Doctor. He was raised in the home of his grandfather (Albert's uncle), and in his autobiographical study *The Words*, Sartre speaks of him as an unpleasant patriarch who "so resembled God the Father that he was often taken for Him." Sartre was not at all favorable to his surroundings and a "grandfather [who] takes pleasure in being a pain in the ass to his sons. That terrible father spent his life crushing them."

But Sartre was to find solace in his loving mother and among books:

> *I began my life as I shall no doubt end it: amidst books. In my grandfather's study there were books everywhere. . . . Though I did not yet know how to read, I already revered those standing stones . . . I felt that our family's prosperity depended on them. I transported myself in a tiny sanctuary, surrounded by*

> *ancient, heavy-set monuments which had seen*
> *me into the world, which would see me out of it,*
> *and whose permanence guaranteed me a future*
> *as calm as the past.* (W, 40-41)

And Sartre would, indeed, find his real purpose among books and writing. He was educated at the famed Ecole Normale Superieure in Paris, where he exhibited very early on an ability for philosophical and literary expression. Among his adult works are the standard philosophical treatises such as the immense work influenced by Husserl and Heidegger titled *Being and Nothingess* (Mary Warnock has called it "a monster of unreadability"), and the much more readable and succinct essay "Existentialism is a Humanism." Among his more creative writings are his many plays such as "No Exit," "Dirty Hands," and "The Respectful Prostitute." Undoubtedly, however, it was his novel *Nausea* which won him greatest acclaim. For this work he was awarded the Nobel Prize in 1964, an award which Sartre publicly refused saying that he did not wish "to become an institution," though it was not always characteristic of Sartre to deflect notoriety.

But Sartre was no bookwormish dweller of the ivory tower. His life was characterized by action and participation (concepts which were to become cornerstones of his brand of existentialism). He fought with his countrymen in World War II, being drafted in 1939. Shortly afterwards he became a German prisoner of war. In prison he continued his studies into Heidegger among others. After his imprisonment he became active in the French Resistance Movement which sought an end to the German occupation of France. Throughout this time, and continuing to the end of his life, he was attracted to Marxist ideals, though he never actually became a member of the Communist party. He was to struggle with Marx's philosophy because, among other reasons, it presented a deterministic perspective which ran counter to Sartre's own adamant commitment to freedom. In his later work *The Critique of Dialectical Reason*, Sartre addresses his relationship to an "existential Marxism."

Though in his philosophical works he often expressed distrust of interpersonal relationships, in his real life he did establish a life-long relationship with Simone de Beauvoir whom he had first met while at the Ecole. Their relationship, though marked by romance, was also somewhat collaborative. Sartre's published works were first read, critiqued, and approved by de Beauvoir, who later established her own reputation as one of France's leading writers and feminists. Let us now turn to some of the key concepts which serve as the foundation for Sartrean existentialism.

Existence Precedes Essence

Perhaps the most widely discussed of Sartre's notions is his claim that "existence precedes essence." This doctrine is most clearly spelled out in his "Existentialism is a Humanism," where he uses it as a defining characteristic of all existentialists. "[T]here are two kinds of existentialists," he explains, "There are, on the one hand, the Christians, amongst whom I shall name Jaspers and Gabriel Marcel, . . . and on the other the existential atheists, amongst whom we must place Heidegger as well as . . . myself. What they have in common is simply the fact that they believe that *existence* comes before *essence* . . . ." Later Sartre argues that the atheistic existentialist holds this doctrine "with greater consistency." And we shall have to consider whether or not Sartre is correct in claiming that the Christian or Religious existentialists hold to the doctrine at all.

What is meant by this doctrine? Sartre uses the analogy of an artisan who manufactures an object—a paper-knife. In the case of making a paper-knife, we clearly have essence preceding existence. The object was first conceived, that is, in the mind of the manufacturer. Its formula, its purpose, its shape, color, dimensions, etc., all of these facts were determined by the creator of the paper-knife before it was brought into existence. The maker of the object had its essence in mind before he had manufactured the object. Now, Sartre continues, let us consider how the human being is different from a paper-knife. For those who believe in "God as the creator" and in "human nature," there really is no difference, he says. For in this view "God makes man according to a procedure and a conception, exactly as the artisan manufactures a paper-knife." According to this idea, essence would precede existence for the human being as well as for objects. Sartre personally, of course, rejects this view:

> *Atheistic existentialism, of which I am a representative, declares with greater consistency that if God does not exist there is at least one being whose existence comes before its essence, a being which exists before it can be defined by any conception of it. That being is man or, as Heidegger has it, the human reality. What do we mean by saying that existence precedes essence? We mean that man first of all exists, encounters himself, surges up in the world—and defines himself afterwards. If man as the*

existentialist sees him is not definable, it is because to begin with he is nothing. He will not be anything until later, and then he will be what he makes of himself. Thus, there is no human nature, because there is no God to have a conception of it. Man simply is. . . . Man is nothing else but that which he makes of himself. That is the first principle of existentialism. (EDS, 349)

Thus Sartre draws the connection between his "existence precedes essence" and his atheism so strongly that one wonders, as we mentioned above, whether we can consider this doctrine as a fundamental defining point for all existentialists, including the Christian or Religious existentialists. We will address this issue again later on.

Absolute Freedom and Responsibility

If each of us is what we make of ourselves, as Sartre contends, it follows that our existence is characterized by a great freedom and responsibility. In *Being and Nothingness* he concludes that we are all "condemned to be free," and that an "absolute responsibility" is "the logical requirement of the consequences of our freedom." But what is the meaning of this irony? How can one be condemned (which suggests a lack of freedom) to be free? In "Existentialism is a Humanism," he explains:

. . . if indeed existence precedes essence, one will never be able to explain one's action by reference to a given and specific human nature; in other words, there is no determinism—man is

free, man is freedom. Nor, on the other hand, if God does not exist, are we provided with any values or commands that could legitimize our behavior. Thus we have neither behind us, nor before us in a luminous realm of values, any means of justification or excuse. We are left alone, without excuse. That is what I mean when I say that man is condemned to be free. Condemned, because he did not create himself, yet is nevertheless at liberty, and from the moment that he is thrown into the world he is responsible for everything he does. (EDS, 353)

When Sartre says that "man *is* freedom" he is suggesting that freedom is the defining characteristic for the human being. In other words, each of us is defined by our freedom; by our choices. Consequently, we are alone in our responsibility for those choices. We cannot pass the buck of responsibility. We are without excuse. Our freedom, then, is a double-edged sword. On the one hand, it is what makes us different from objects—it is our subjectivity—and we are conscious of this as a remarkable defining condition of who we are as distinct from mere things. But we cannot escape the consequences of our freedom. For Sartre, we not only choose for ourselves, *we literally choose ourselves.* We create ourselves with the choices that we make. But more about this later.

Inauthentic Choices: Self-Deception and Bad Faith

While each of us is utterly free and responsible for our freedom, not all choices are equal for Sartre. It is possible, in other words, to make bad choices and to exist in a state that he refers to as "bad faith" (*mauvaise foi*). One who is in bad faith has made inauthentic choices and is involved in self-deception. In *Being and Nothingness*, in fact, Sartre characterizes bad faith as a "lie to oneself." But what is the lie about? How is such a person deceived? Sartre reveals several patterns for us, but all of them reflect some basic features. The one who is in bad faith flees from responsibility and hides behind excuses. If I am unhappy with my life or of any particular aspect of it, and if I blame my past, my environment, my genes, my parenting, my passions, in short, if I blame everything except myself, I am in bad faith. Bad faith is a non-acceptance of the fact that I am truly free and alone in my responsibility for my choices. Sartre does recognize that there are things outside of our control. It is true, he denies a human nature, but he admits to a *human condition* and to what he calls "facticity"—a set of facts about myself that were determined for me (my sex, my nationality, my geography, my parentage, etc.). But Sartre's commitment to an absolute freedom will not allow one to use those things as an excuse for our lives. Sartre makes the very telling point in many places, but perhaps most strikingly in "Dirty Hands," that *we cannot change our past, but we can change what our past means*. One who is a product of an abusive upbringing, for example, cannot erase that abuse, to be sure. But one is faced with a choice: to use that abuse as an excuse for all present failures, or to attempt to overcome that past and escape the cycle of abuse for myself.

One particular form of bad faith discussed by Sartre is the act of role-playing. So often we hide behind the masks offered to us by society (remember discussions from chapter one, and Rousseau's discussion here). We are too often tempted to disguise our true selves behind the facades which are socially acceptable. And often we become so involved in the act, that we are no longer even aware that we are playing a role. Sartrean existentialism requires us to remove the mask of inauthenticity and to reveal our true selves in our acts—those that we have chosen for ourselves, and for which we alone accept responsibility.

Sartre and Creativity

Human creation replaces the dead god

In *Being and Nothingness*, Sartre says that "Human reality is the pure effort to become God . . . ." Formerly it was God who was seen as the Creator of man, now man must make himself—he must become his own God, his own creator. And formerly beauty was seen as evidence for God—the beauty exhibited in the universe itself seemed to call for a Divine Artist, as the teleological (from the Gk: *telos*=end, purpose, goal) argument intends to show. In his essay "Art and Salvation," Sartre argues that beauty was formerly used to support a *theodicy* (a justification for belief in God), but now, according to Sartre, beauty will support an *anthropodicy* (a justification for belief in man):

> Formerly the beautiful was an integral part of theodicy: the artist "showed" God his work as the enfeoffed vassal showed his lord his fief which the latter had just given him; . . . Today God is dead, even in the heart of the believer, and art becomes an anthropodicy: it makes man believe that man created the world; it presents his work to him and justifies his having made it . . . . (PJPS, 405)

Human creation is ex-nihilo

According to the medieval Saint Augustine, as we have seen, God created the universe *ex-nihilo*—out of nothing. According to Sartre, the human artist, too, creates from nothingness. Roquentin, the main character in Sartre's *Nausea*, says of himself: "*I am the one* who pulls myself from the nothingness . . . " This "nothingness" spoken of by Roquentin, is the same "nothingness" talked about in "Existentialism is a Humanism," and *Being and Nothingness*. It contains the whole list of "nothings"—*no* God, *no* purpose, *no* human nature, *no* preordained values, *no* determinism, *no* excuses. And Roquentin is not merely just another character for Sartre. In *The Words*, Sartre says that "I *was* Roquentin; I used him to show, without complacency, the texture of my life."

There is a striking similarity here between Augustine and Sartre concerning *ex-nihilo* creation. They seem both to be after the same point: i.e., creation, in order to be true creation, must be free.

Augustine argued that if God created out of something rather than nothing, His freedom would be limited—and thus not really free at all. If God created the universe out of something (some pre-existing material) rather than nothing, then either His freedom was curtailed because He was unable (hence, unfree) to create out of nothing, or because of the defects contained within the pre-existing material itself. In either case, God's freedom becomes questioned. Sartre seems to be suggesting the same here for human creation: in order to be truly free, our creations must be from nothingness. To be truly *ours*, our creations must emerge from nothingness by our own acts.

We create our selves, our meaning, and our values

As he reports in *The Words*, Sartre had an experience of self-creation as a very young man: "I keep creating myself; I am the giver and the gift." And later in the same work he recognizes that it is precisely in his own artistry—as a writer—that "the Giver can be transformed into his own Gift . . . ." For Sartre, the product of our creation is ourselves. In creation, we are the givers and the receivers. This is the meaning of his "Man is what he makes of himself." And it is in our *projects*—in our creative acts—that we create ourselves. *In Search for a Method* Sartre tells us that "Only the project . . . can account for . . . *human creativity*. It is necessary to choose." He goes on to say that "Man defines himself by his project."

And, as Sartre says in "Existentialism is a Humanism," since there is no God, there is no "possibility of finding values in an intelligible heaven." We are not "provided with any values or commands . . . ." We must, therefore, choose and create our own values. Thus the human being truly replaces the dead God. We create ourselves, we create our values. We determine, therefore, the meaning of our own lives.

Marcel's Critique of Sartre

Marcel's attitude towards creativity, especially when it involves value and meaning in our lives, is diametrically opposed to Sartre's. Let us look briefly at his critique.

Values are neither created nor chosen

In *Mass Against Mass Society* Marcel challenges Sartre's notion that values are chosen and created by us. For Marcel, this view of Sartre's is a "serious error . . . 'value' is essentially something which *cannot* be chosen." In *The Philosophy of Existentialism* Marcel explains his own position: "I find that I do not 'choose' my values at all, but that I recognize them . . . ."

Marcel supports his critique by providing an argument which questions the internal consistency of Sartre's position. Sartre has argued that because there is no God, there can be no intrinsic, inherent, or objective value to any choices we make. There is no objective backdrop of standards to compare our chosen values to. Yet Sartre, as we have seen above, distinguishes between authentic and inauthentic ("bad faith") choices. Marcel specifically criticizes the consistency of Sartre for praising the "authentic" choices of the heroes of the French Resistance (the movement he himself participated in) for example, while denigrating the "inauthentic" and "misguided" choices of others:

> *Now I ask you in the name of what principle, having first denied the existence of values or at least of their objective basis, can he establish any appreciable difference between those utterly misguided but undoubtedly courageous men who joined voluntarily the Anti-Bolshevik Legion, on the one hand, and the heroes of the Resistance movement on the other? I see no way of establishing the difference without admitting that causes have their intrinsic value and, consequently, that values are real.* (PE, 87)

And earlier in the same work Marcel criticizes the internal consistency of Sartre's position by pointing out that the whole concept of "bad faith" implies an opposite choice, i.e., a sincere or "good faith" choice among competing values. Or else, what can "bad faith" mean?: "Bad faith," Marcel argues, "cannot be defined, it cannot assume its specific character except by opposition to sincerity."

The artist is a receiver as well as a giver

Sartre's error, according to Marcel, lies essentially in his inability or unwillingness to admit to the idea of receptivity. For Sartre, we are only givers: we give meaning to our lives through the choices that only we give to ourselves without help, and without excuse. We are what we make of ourselves and what we give to ourselves.

But true creation, for Marcel, involves the recognition of reception as well as of giving. We must begin, he says, by realizing that our very existence is not something we give to ourselves, but a gift:

> *Each one of us is in a position to recognize that his own essence is a gift . . . ; that he himself is a gift, and that he has no existence at all through himself.* (MB II, 173)

This is a direct challenge to Sartre's "Man is what he makes of himself." It is also a rejection of the Sartrean "existence precedes essence." For Marcel, there is also a mysterious presence and reality which precedes our existence also. He discusses this in *The Mystery of Being*, part one, where he says that we are all part of a "reality which is conferred upon us or in which we participate." And it is the whole notion of participation, according to Marcel, that Sartre has no comprehension of. For Marcel, this is Sartre's ultimate blindness, or his ultimate refusal (one cannot know for certain which it is), i.e., Sartre's philosophy is developed from the point of view of the spectator. In *The Philosophy of Existence* Marcel says that "Sartre's world is the world as seen from the terrace of a *cafe'*." And Marcel goes on to point out that Sartre has accepted this characterization. Certainly Sartre's *Being and Nothingness* is filled with the language of spectatorship. To be convinced of this, one need only examine his extensive analysis in this work of "The Look," for example, which provides the backdrop of spectatorship. Just how diametrically opposed Marcel and Sartre are on this score, is evidenced when we recall that for Marcel, true relations with others; the true "we" for Marcel, requires participation and the rejection of spectatorship. Sartre, on the other hand, argues that "The best example of the 'we' can be furnished us by the spectator at a theatrical performance . . . ."

Sartre's rejection of participation for spectatorship seems part and parcel of his desire for absolute freedom. If I am a spectator I am free to get involved, or simply to move on to the next spectacle. The same motivation, Marcel argues, lies behind Sartre's refusal to admit the idea of reception into his philosophy. "[F]or Sartre," he says in *The Philosophy of Existence*, "to receive is incompatible with being free; indeed, a being who is free is bound to deny to himself that he has received anything." From Marcel's point of view, Sartre himself seems resigned to suffer the fate of "Inez," one of his own characters in "No Exit," who proclaims; "I'm all dried up. I can't give and I can't receive."

But true creation, argues Marcel, cannot take place without the union of giving and receiving. In his *Existential Background of Human Dignity*, he says that "creation is a response to a call received . . . ." And in *Creative Fidelity*, Marcel elaborates:

> . . . to receive in this context is to open myself to, hence to give myself . . . . We already encounter at this level the paradox which is at the core of creation itself . . . . The Artist seems to be nourished by the very thing he seeks to incarnate; hence the identification of receiving and giving is ultimately realized in him. (CF, 91-92)

Receiving and giving are therefore not only unified, but identified in the act of creation. For Marcel then, we do not make ourselves from blank slates; we do not bring ourselves into existence out of nothing. Creation, at least human creation, is not *ex nihilo*. We are both givers and receivers.

Critique and Comments

In comparing Marcel and Sartre, we have picked up again the theme which we encountered at the end of our discussion concerning Kierkegaard and Nietzsche. Marcel and Sartre really do seem to carry on the argument begun before them by these two great "fathers" of existentialism. We have, on the one hand, Nietzsche and Sartre who argue that we must become godlike in our creation—i.e., it must be *ex nihilo*. Kierkegaard and Marcel, on the other hand, deny that human creation is *ex nihilo*. In essence, the point of view of religious existentialism is that *we neither have the ability nor the need to become divine artists*—i.e., human creation is unique and different from the divine. The human artist literally cannot imitate the divine creative act. This kind of act would require a type of omnipotence reserved only for God (Marcel would even argue that it is reserved only for an image of God which is inevitably false and artificial). But humans are in no way omnipotent. We do not and we cannot create from nothing. We begin our creations from many givens: our world, our experiences, indeed, our very lives. This inability to be omnipotent is no loss for us. We humans do not need to create from nothing—ours is still a wondrous and mysterious form of freedom and creativity; it is *human* freedom and *human* creativity.

To think otherwise about human creation, it seems, and to demand that it be *ex nihilo* and absolute in order to be really free and meaningful, is to hold to a very naive misconception about the nature of human freedom. This is the point of view which argues that freedom, in order really to be freedom, must be *freedom from*; i.e., freedom from all constraints and boundaries. But it would appear that freedom which is totally limitless is not freedom at all. Rather, it would become a manifestation of chaos and purposelessness. Meaningful freedom, it would appear, needs to be *freedom to*, rather than freedom from. And *the freedom to* do anything whatever requires one to operate within a given context—to both receive this context and to give (to contribute) to this context. This seems to be an essential component of meaningful freedom and creativity.

Let us attempt a few brief examples. In every aspect of life there are those who seem to rise above. In the area of sports, for example, we can think of the incredible abilities of a Michael Jordan, possibly the greatest basketball player in the history of the sport. Jordan exhibits freedom and creativity within the game of basketball on a superstar level. But imagine if Michael Jordan attempted to become even more free and creative by simply ignoring the rules and boundaries of the game. Suppose, for instance, that he claimed the right to double-dribble whenever he felt like it, or to not dribble at all and to therefore carry the basketball as if he were playing football rather than basketball. Or suppose that he wanted the right to shoot into the opponent's basket and to have the points count for his side. One could imagine many other such requests. One can also easily imagine why they would be denied. For these requests or demands would be tantamount to the request not to play basketball at all. In order to play basketball, one needs to really play it within the context of what the game really is and means—this would, of course, include all of the rules and boundaries that make the game meaningful.

In order to participate in any meaningful way, one must receive the rules of the game and play within them. This is true not only for basketball, but it would appear to be true (though in varying degrees) for any human activity. Consider a Horowitz at the piano. Does his great creativity on that instrument not involve a given context? Has he not mastered this context? Is this not why he is a master of that beautiful music? Consider a Michelangelo and his sculpting artistry. Is he not bound by a context here? Yet is he not free to create beauty from what he is given? His artistry seems not to be constrained (beyond the limits of freedom) by the particular defects of his marble, nor by the human limitations of his hands and tools. Michelangelo does not demand to be god before he can be an artist.

This theory of creation offered by Marcel and which I shall heretofore refer to as "Marcellian Creation," (the view that human creativity is a *freedom to* rather than a *freedom from*, and that human creativity is not *ex nihilo* but receives what it is given and creates within that context) seems to be true to our common human experience. It also seems true to the reflections of the great artists, from the Classical, to the Romantics and beyond. It is also true to the reflections of Carl Jung, to whom we shall now turn.

Selected Bibliography for Chapter Eight

Gallagher, Kenneth T.: *The Philosophy of Gabriel Marcel*. Fordham University Press, New York, 1962.

Marcel Gabriel: *Being and Having.*   Harper Torchbooks, New York, 1965.

——————: *Creative Fidelity*. The Noonday Press, New York, 1964. Abbreviated (CF).

——————: *Homo Viator.*   Harper Torchbooks, New York, 1962.

——————: *Philosophical Fragments.*   University of Notre Dame Press, Indiana, 1965.

——————:*Presence and Immortality.*   Duquesne University Press, Pittsburgh, 1967.

——————: *Problematic Man.* Herder and Herder, New York, 1967.

——————: *Searchings.*   Newman Press, New York, 1967.

——————: *The Mystery of Being*, Volumes I and II. University Press of America, Lanham, 1978. Abbreviated (MB).

——————: *The Philosophy of Existentialism.* Citadel Press, New Jersey, 1956. Abbreviated (PE).

Sartre, Jean Paul: *Anti-Semite and Jew.*   Schocken Books, New York, 1965.

—————: *Art and Salvation.* Published in Robert Dennon Cumming, *The Philosophy of Jean Paul Sartre.* Vintage Books, New York, 1972. Abbreviated (PJPS).

—————: *Being and Nothingness.* Philosophical Library, New York, 1956.

—————: "Existentialism is a Humanism." Published in Walter Kaufmann, *Existentialism from Dostoevsky to Sartre.* New American Library, New York, 1975. Abbreviated (EDS).

—————: *Nausea.* New Directions, New York, 1964.

—————: *No Exit and Three Other Plays.* Vintage Books, New York, 1955.

—————: *Search for a Method.* Vintage Books, New York, 1963.

—————: *The Words.* George Braziller, New York, 1964. Abbreviated (W).

Warnock, Mary: *The Philosophy of Sartre.* Hutchinson University Library, London, 1965.

Chapter 9

The Challenge of Postmodernism

We have now encountered specific concepts of creativity. As it is applied to the human enterprise of creating a meaningful life, we have arrived at an understanding of creation as a combination of giving and receiving. This notion is found in Plato: Beauty and Goodness are changeless essences that we can receive and use as standards for measuring particular beautiful and good things. It is also found in Augustine's reflections on Divine creation (only God is an *ex nihilo* creator). It was embodied in Michelangelo's work "The Captives," and in Wordworth's "creator and receiver both." And it became a major focal point in the evaluation of Kierkegaard versus Nietzsche, and Marcel versus Sartre. It appears, that is, that the views of Nietzsche and Sartre raise the specter of inconsistency—how can one legitimately reject "slave mentality" (as Nietzsche wishes to do), or "bad faith" (as Sartre does), when there is no standard (because "God is dead") against which these may be measured? Why should the slave reject his slavery? Why should one living in "bad faith" be moved in another direction? Each makes his own choices and standards. If others are critical of him, then they are critical from their own point of view, and their own standards—standards which he does not accept.

We saw that in order to legitimate any rejection of these ways of living, one seems required to postulate a *given* (something which we receive and do not create). This is what allows Kierkegaard to spurn the esthete and the ethical, in favor of the religious stage. It is what enables Marcel to eschew spectatorship, and to advocate a participatory mode of existence.

In short, we are moved to reject the *classical relativism* offered by the sophist Protagoras (c. 490- 420 B.C.). Protagoras' famous words are that "Man is the measure of all things . . . ." Each one, according to this view, decides for himself what is true, beautiful, and good. In applying this to our quest for meaning, we could say that classical relativism implies (as do Nietzsche and Sartre) that we are each the sole creators (*ex nihilo*) of our own meaning. But this view offers the same inconsistency challenged above. By what right, then, would we criticize those members of society who make the "wrong" choices (e.g., Nietzsche's "slave")? Indeed, what would the word "wrong" mean? For the classical relativist, each person must decide for himself what is "right" and "wrong," "true" or "false." There is no standard lying outside the individual (or his society). Under classical relativism we are each godlike creators of our own standards.

Postmodernism

As we begin a new century, the old argument of classical relativism has been revised and reformulated by *postmodernism*. In philosophy, postmodernism refers to the views held to by such French intellectuals as Michel Foucault (1926-1984), Jacques Derrida (b. 1930), and Jean-François Lyotard (b. 1924). There are many other thinkers who share a family resemblance with postmodernism, including the American pragmatist Richard Rorty (b. 1931). What postmodernism offers is a rejection of "modernism," described as a belief in truth (e. g., the belief that there is one true reality or picture of reality), and as a belief that knowledge is possible (i. e., the human mind can achieve absolute and objective knowledge of that reality). According to postmodernism, we must give up the search for truth with a capital "T." That search is a vestige of modernism. As Lyotard puts it, we must abandon our "nostalgia of the whole and the one . . . ." (L, 564) In this respect, postmodernism bears striking similarity to Albert Camus' existentialism. In *The Myth of Sisyphus*, for example, Camus speaks of and rejects the "nostalgia for unity, that appetite for the absolute . . . ." (C, 13) But why must we abandon this nostalgia?

Postmodernists believe that all "truths" offered by individuals (or societies) are bound to and are therefore biased by the particular frameworks (cultural, social, religious, psychological, scientific, etc.) dominant in that individual's world. In short, one can never escape these frameworks; never adopt a stance above or outside them in order to "see" the truth objectively. Indeed, "truth" is not there to be seen at all, it is, rather, a perspective, a point of view—all truth is interpretation based on this perspectivalism. The mind does not "mirror" reality, it makes reality (out of the clay it has available—culture, society, etc.). In this respect, postmodernism is an extension of the projects of Nietzsche and Sartre. Like them, postmodernism rejects any given that we could receive. We (as prisoners of our own frameworks) are total givers—we create truth and meaning *ex nihilo*.

Postmodernism would therefore be subject to the same criticism as Nietzsche/Sartre. How can postmodernism validly reject positions as "untrue"? How can postmodernism reject Nazism, for instance, or any form of injustice? How can postmodernism oppose bigotry and hatred, totalitarianism and dogmatism?

It appears that postmodernism has the same shortcomings as classical relativism. Indeed, it is reasonable to ask whether there is any substantial difference between these two views. Postmodernists do accept at least some form of relativism. Rorty, operating from the tradition of pragmatism (seen as a supporter of the postmodern rejection of Platonism or objective Truth), attempts to address what he takes to be a very important difference between pragmatism/postmodernism and what he calls "vulgar relativism." Vulgar relativism is described as a "jejune indifference to argument and inquiry" which holds that "every view is as good as every other." Rorty rejects this view. We can assert, he believes, that our creations, our views, our traditions, are not mere arbitrary choices (only as good as any other creations, views, and traditions), and still avoid both "the Scylla of Platonism and the Charybdis of vulgar relativism."

> *The difference between vulgar relativism and pragmatism is that pragmatism says that the fact that a view is* ours—our *language's,* our *tradition's,* our *culture's, is an excellent* prima facie *reason for holding it. It is not, of course, a knock-down argument against competing views. But it does put the burden of proof on such views. It says that rationality consists in a decent respect for the opinions . . . of mankind. . . . pragmatism [provides a way to guide people] between the Scylla of Platonism and the Charybdis of vulgar relativism. This comes down to the problem of getting them to realize that our having no organ for truth, no Reason in the Platonic sense, does not mean that everything must be turned over to the emotions. Or, to put it another way, it is the problem of realizing that there is a middle way between reliance on a God-surrogate and on one's individual preferences—namely, reliance on the common sense of the community to which one belongs.* (R, 527)

Rorty is objecting to Platonism (but also to the views we have traced in thinkers like Augustine, Michelangelo, Rousseau, Coleridge, Wordsworth, Kierkegaard, and Marcel) as symbolic of the position that there is a given; a truth that we all are able to receive (through our "Reason" he says,—though Rousseau and Kierkegaard would say that we receive it from non-rational avenues). He supports the Nietzschean/Sartrean view that we are the sole (*ex nihilo*) creators of *our* truths, *our* traditions, *our* cultures (his emphasis on "ours" underscores their *ex nihilo* quality). And we can still avoid, he thinks, the charge of vulgar relativism. But can we?

If we are to oppose vulgar relativism, it seems that we must be equipped with the ability to say, for example, that views like Nazism are unacceptable. And it seems that we must be able to oppose views like this *not* simply within the temporary/fleeting aspects of a given culture ("Nazism is wrong, at least in this period of history, and from *our* cultural/social point of view."), but with some manner of force ("Nazism is wrong, for this world, and for any just world!"). Nietzsche rejects slave mentality, and Sartre rejects bad faith, not from any limited standpoint, they reject them pure and simple (for all worlds). How can they consistently do so? This problem is unresolved by postmodernism. How can pragmatism/postmodernism consistently reject views such as Nazism, since to reject them is to say, in fact, that they are untrue (again, not just from a particular point of view, but untrue period)?

We want the ability to say to Nazism (and to all forms of intolerance) that it is wrong! That it may be a creation, but that it is a very bad creation! Postmodernism seems no more equipped than vulgar relativism to do this. This is because both vulgar relativism and postmodernism maintain an *ex nihilo* theory of choice and creation. *Our* cultures and traditions, *our* truths, they say, are *our* creations (this language is reminiscent of Sartre's "Man is what he makes of himself"). These choices are not based on some given truths that are available to us. In short, vulgar relativism and postmodernism agree with the

Nietzschean/Sartrean view that man is a giver (*ex nihilo* creator) only, and not a receiver of truth. The Nietzschean/Sartrean problem, however, remains. If each one is a sole giver/chooser of truth, how can one choice be rejected over any other? The problem is that the Nazi can argue that from *his* view, *his*, culture, *his* tradition, it is not wrong to perpetrate mass destruction on a whole race of people. What can postmodernism say to this? With what force can it maintain any rejection?

The problem is that when we believe, as postmodernism seems to, that we choose our values *ex nihilo* (remember, this is the key debate between Marcel and Sartre—Marcel argued that 'value' is essentially something which *cannot* be chosen.), then those choices truly are arbitrary, and therefore it is difficult to avoid vulgar relativism's "all values are equal." And what is even more telling, if values (such as the value of opposing Nazism) are chosen *ex nihilo*, it would appear that a culture or individual would equally have had the opportunity of choosing the opposite value as well. What would it be like to live in a world wherein the values of hatred, deceit, and intolerance were chosen over those of love, honesty, and tolerance? Had our culture's choices been different, according to postmodernism, we could very well be now exalting hatred over love, deceit over honesty, and intolerance over tolerance.

But this seems utterly unacceptable. The postmodernist no doubt would respond that it seems unacceptable only because we are prisoners of a culture which has chosen certain values. But it seems that hatred, dishonesty and intolerance are false in and of themselves. It does not appear that they are false simply because our culture made value choices inconsistent with them (indeed, some cultures have not, e.g., Nazi culture).   If our or any culture chooses the values of hatred, we feel bound to express a rejection of that culture as unjust (even when that culture is our own—as expressed in civil disobedience).   And we would use the principles of justice (as given to us) as our standard. We would not reject hatred as an *ex nihilo* choice, but as something inconsistent with a value (justice) that we do not create at all.   Rather, we *recognize* justice as a value (remember Marcel's statement: "I find that I do not 'choose' my values at all, but I recognize them . . . ."). In short, we are receivers of values. And in accepting this reception, we create our responses to hatred (here we are givers as well as receivers).

It appears, then, that postmodernism has no more power than vulgar relativism to defend one choice over the other.   But we seem to feel, with the force of what Kierkegaard called "subjective truth," that some choices are better and worse than others. Love is better than hatred.   Honesty is better than dishonesty. Tolerance is better than intolerance.

It appears that even the postmodernists, ultimately, agree that love, honesty, and tolerance are values which should be promoted above their opposites.   Foucault and Derrida, for instance, offer profound rejections of intolerance (such as homophobia and Nazism) in their major writings. The question is, how consistently can they agree with the promotion of tolerance against intolerance? Postmodernism has been summarized by scholars of that movement as holding to "the key assumption that . . . there is nothing outside contingent discourses to which a discourse of values can be grounded—no eternal truths, no universal human experience, no universal human rights . . . ." (F, 8). But scholars have also noted that key postmodern thinkers have not always consistently held to this kind of relativism, finding it "remarkable [for instance] that both Foucault and Derrida arrive, at the end of their trajectories, at an affirmation of one law above all others. That law is effectively the categorical imperative that human beings should never be treated as means alone, that the foundation of right behaviour is to be sought in the idea of universalizability of the principles according to which one acts." (B, 2)

Clearly Foucault and Derrida would affirm this Kantian ethics as "truer" than, say, a Hitlerian ethics which promotes the use of people (indeed, whole races of people) as mere means to the Nazi end. And there seems to be a connection between these truths felt on the ethical plane, and those of aesthetics as well. For Michelangelo's Sistine Chapel is certainly better than a school boy's scribblings on a wall. And when we say "better," we mean that it is better pure and simple. We do not mean it is better only from a particular cultural perspective—it is simply better! And if Michelangelo's work is better, it appears that it must be so by more closely approximating truth, beauty, and goodness. Truth, beauty and goodness, are here seen as standards (in the Platonic sense) we can use (they are given to us) to judge better versus worse creations.

It is true that these standards do not admit of proof. As Aristotle would say, they are held to in the form of an intuition. They are first principles— starting points, not ending points. They are first principles because other principles are derived from them. And first principles cannot be "proven" since in order to do so, one would have to derive them from other principles, in which case they would become secondary principles. They are principles, as Kierkegaard would say, that we *feel* (subjective truths). And Marcel would remind us that feeling is not passive receptivity, it is both a giving and a receiving.

Selected Bibliography for Chapter Nine

Boyne, Roy: *Foucault and Derrida: The Other Side of Reason.* Unwin Hyman Press, London, 1990. Abbreviated as (B).

Camus, Albert: *The Myth of Sisyphus and Other Essays.* Vintage Books, New York, 1955. Abbreviated as (C).

Faigley, Lester: *Fragments of Rationality: Postmodernity and the Subject of Composition.* University of Pittsburgh Press, Pittsburgh, PA, 1992. Abbreviated as (F).

Lawhead, William: "Rethinking Philosophy: Postmodernism," in his *The Voyage of Discovery: A History of Western Philosophy* (pp. 579-584). Wadsworth, Belmont, California, 1996.

Lyotard, Jean-François: "What is Postmodernism?," printed in *Art and Its Significance*, Stephen David Ross (editor). State University of New York Press, New York, 1994, pp.561-565. Abbreviated as (L).

Rorty, Richard: "Hermeneutics, General Studies, and Teaching," printed in *Classic and Contemporary Readings in the Philosophy of Education* (pp. 522-536), edited by Steven M. Cahn. McGraw Hill, New York, 1997. Abbreviated as (R).

Part Two

Profiles of Creative Genius

In part two we explore examples of creative genius in the lives and works of Mozart, Beethoven, Dickinson, Van Gogh, Wilde, Wright, and Jung.

Chapter 10

Mozart and Beethoven: Two Faces of Musical Genius

The praise and adulation given to Mozart is nearly incomparable throughout history. Mozart scholar Paul Henry Lang has written that the "elements of Mozart's greatness are beyond analysis and discussion. Other musicians can be discussed, but his music does not offer any opening—it is pure, unbroken, finished to the very end. There is no such harmonious phenomenon in the entire history of music." Such unparalleled praise flows abundant from scholars and historians of Mozart. Listen to Friedrich Kerst's words: "Mozart! What a radiance streams from the name! Bright and pure as the light of the sun, Mozart's music greets us. . . . Mozart was a child of the Sun." And if the words of scholars and historians are not enough, consider these words from none other than Goethe, Germany's greatest poet:

> *What else is genius than that productive power through which deeds arise, worthy of standing in the presence of God and Nature, and which, for this reason, bear results and are lasting? All the creations of Mozart are in this*

class; within them there is a generative force which is transplanted from generation to generation, and it is not likely soon to be exhausted or devoured. (K, 3)

Wolfgang Amadeus Mozart

was born in Salzburg, Austria, in 1756, the son of Leopold who was a skilled violinist and court musician to the Archbishop of Salzburg. Leopold had also become known for his publications in musical theory and practice; the Mozart name, therefore, had already earned respect and admiration among musicians. And Leopold set out to educate his own children in the art of music. Maria Anna, Wolfgang's older sister, was instructed on the clavier (an early precursor of the piano) by age 7, and she earned a reputation as an excellent performer. Maria and Wolfgang were the only two survivors of seven children. Little Wolfgang, beginning at the age of 2 and 3, was constantly at his sister's side and listened intently to the music lessons. He showed promise at

an extremely early age—he could follow concertos
from pure memory, and at 4 he began to compose his
own pieces.   He was an acutely intelligent boy who
loved mathematical and musical games, and who had
a marked need to be appreciated and loved.   As his
reputation developed, everyone loved the *wunderkint.*
The Emperor Francis called him "the little magician"
and loved to play musical games with him. Yet all the
praise and applause that came to him so early did not
seem to adversely affect him—by all testimony he
remained a normal, passionate, obedient child, with a
passionate heart for people and his art.   Fittingly, the
mature Mozart was to later echo the Romantic belief
that "It is the heart that confers the patent of nobility
on man." (K, 55)   However, he also later recognized,
like Plato, that the passions must be controlled in art:

> . . . *the passions, whether violent or not, must
> never be carried in their expression to the verge
> of disgust, and music, even in the most awful
> situations, must not offend the ear but always
> please, consequently always remain music . . . .*
> (K, 21)

Leopold paraded the young boy (along with his
sister) throughout Germany, France and England.
Mozart was able to play the music of such giants as
Bach and Handel at sight and with perfect precision,
exact timing and style.   After the first few years,
however, the Mozarts experienced a declining novelty.
There were always money difficulties, and obligations
to the Archbishop of Salzburg kept the family from the
full freedom desired.   This left Leopold in much
anxiety, though the children remained good-natured
and happy.

Mozart biographers have given ample testimony to the brilliance of his memory, power of concentration, and most of all, speed. His ability to produce at a rapid rate is recognized by Mozart himself, when in a letter to his father he wrote "What would at other times require fourteen days to write, I could do now in four. I composed in one day Adamberger's aria in A, Cavalieri's in B-flat, and the trio, and copied them out in a day and a half." (L, 19) There are likewise reports of Mozart composing dance pieces one hour before their performance for Count Pachta. Erich Hertzmann argues that "Mozart must have had a photographic memory and could compose music faster than his pen would write. He must have worked out many compositions in his head before he sat down to put them on paper. The tale that he composed the overture to *Don Giovanni* the night before the performance gains credibility if we assume that the whole piece was worked out in his mind beforehand. He copied the music from the imaginary score which he knew by heart."

Yet Mozart's talent was hard worked for. Edward Lowinsky says that "Mozart's rhythmic genius was be no means a gift laid in the cradle by a smiling Muse." Mozart himself may disagree. He recognized the incontestable fact of his "gift," since he talks about the "talent for composition which a kind God gave me in such generous measure." (K, 50) But Mozart matched the gift with hard work on his own part (in doing so, he embodies the theory of creativity we have seen defended by Marcel—creation is a giving as well as a receiving). He benefited, to begin with, from an upbringing which encouraged the importance of the arts and music in particular. And beginning with his early lessons from his father, Mozart was able to see the value of hard work. He speaks of this value in his letters:

> . . . *it is a mistake to think that the practise of my art has come easy to me. I assure you, dear friend, no one has given so much care to the study of composition as I. There is scarcely a famous master in music whose works I have not frequently and diligently studied.* (K, 6)

In particular, scholars such as Ernst Fritz Schmid have noted the important influence on Mozart from the older master Joseph Haydn. Later the influence became mutual. The two artists met for the first time in the 1780's. Mozart's *Figaro* so impressed Haydn that, according to Schmid, it "haunted his dreams . . . he gallantly and with full conviction abandoned the field of opera to Mozart." In a letter Haydn remarks: " . . . hardly anyone could expect to be the equal of the great Mozart . . . If I could only impress the inimitable works of Mozart on the souls of all music-lovers and especially of the great men of this world and with the same deep musical understanding and the same great emotion with which my soul receives them; the nations would vie for the possession of such a jewel." (L, 96)

Mozart fell in love with Constance Weber, a talented singer he had worked with. Holmes describes her as a singer of "very considerable powers and great taste. She possessed a real insight into the art, and was a competent judge of most of that in which her future husband excelled." The two were married and lived in relative happiness with their six children. The last years of Mozart are an unhappy story, however, for he became a man filled with illness and debt. In 1787, he was hurt by the death of his father, and scholars such as Stanley Sadie point out that his "resigned attitude to death undoubtedly coloured the music of his last years, and it is arguable that his own end was hastened by his ready, even willing, acknowledgment of its inevitability." Lang suggests that Mozart had from his youth a sort of Romantic attitude towards death. In an early letter to his father, Mozart states that ". . . death, when we come to consider it closely, is the true goal of our existence . . . ." (L, 14) In one of his last letters to his father, Mozart speaks of death:

> *Young as I am, I never go to bed without thinking that possibly I may not be alive on the morrow; yet no one of the many persons who know me can say I am morose or melancholy. For this happy disposition I thank my Creator daily, and wish all my heart that it were shared by all my fellows.* (K, 67)

When Mozart approached his final years, he became even more absorbed in the magic of his music. The same year his father died, he worked on *Don Giovanni*, and *Eine Kleine Nacht Music*, among others. The *Requiem* was his final composition, a work which consumed him in a feverish way. Eric Blom tells us that "it often depressed him like a premonition of death." On the day of his death (the 5th of December, 1791) Mozart told his friends, eerily, "Did I not tell you that I was composing this 'Requiem' for myself." (K, 86)

Mozart's precise ailment is unknown. Rheumatic fever, Bright's disease, brain inflammation, have all been posthumously postulated. Mozart himself believed that he had been poisoned by an Italian rival named Salieri (this was a story line in the feature film "Amadeus," though there appears to be no real evidence of this apart from rumor and innuendo).

The young Mozart died at the age of 35, in a state of regret. As he lay dying, and while friends sang to him portions of his *Requiem*, he uttered the following words:

> *And now I must go just as it had become possible for me to live quietly. Now I must leave my art just as I had freed myself from the slavery of fashion, had broken the bonds of speculators, and won the privilege of following my own feelings and composing freely and independently whatever my heart prompted! I must away from my family, from my poor children in the moment when I should have been able better to care for their welfare!* (K, 87)

His funeral, as Edward Holmes suggests, "was unostentatious to meanness, and far from such as befitted the obsequies of so great a man." The remains were deposited in a common and undistinguished pauper's grave. Mozart's remains were left there and almost forgotten to history; the actual position of his grave is still unknown.

Several years before his death, in the spring of 1787, a remarkable event occurred in Mozart's life, though he could have scarcely known how remarkable it was. On this occasion, a young man embarking on his own musical career was introduced to him during a visit to Vienna. During the interview Mozart

listened to the young musician's performance and was
greatly impressed by it.   But thinking that this
performance may have been only a narrow example of
the young man's talent, he tested him by giving him
an unknown theme to improvise upon.   The young
man began an improvisation which so impressed
Mozart, that he proclaimed to his friends waiting in an
adjoining room: "This young man will some day make
a noise heard throughout the world."   The young
man's name was Ludwig Van Beethoven.

Ludwig Van Beethoven

was born in Bonn, Germany in 1770 (the same year
that William Wordsworth was born in England).   His
father, Johann van Beethoven, plagued the family
with his severe drinking and constantly put the family
in financial trouble.   Johann had been instructed by
his father in the violin and piano, and he passed this
tradition on to his own children (there were three
survivors from an original six children: Ludwig, Karl,
and Nicholas).   From the beginning, it was clear that

the only promising musician among them was Ludwig. Beethoven scholar John N. Burk points out that "the boy took to his notes so naturally that his parent was reminded of the recent fruitful exploitation of the infant Mozart."

The comparison to Mozart, therefore, began early and continued throughout Beethoven's career. As an adult Beethoven reported in his journals that "I have always reckoned myself among the greatest admirers of Mozart, and shall do so till the day of my death." (FK, 55). In 1792 he was provided the opportunity to study under Joseph Haydn in Vienna. As Joseph Schmidt-Gorg points out, this became possible due to help from his friend Count Waldstein who stated in a letter to Beethoven "Through uninterrupted industry receive Mozart's spirit from the hands of Haydn." In 1799 Beethoven attended a performance of Mozart's C minor concerto and said to a fellow composer "we'll never be in a position to make the like of that!" (S, 44).

Johann was truly moved by the young Ludwig's talent. He quickly began showcasing the child prodigy. In preparation, Johann's demands on the boy increased. Ludwig's daily lessons were severe and prolonged. The Beethoven's landlords recall the child being placed under such a punishing regiment that it left him weeping.

Ludwig's academic studies took second place to his music. As he grew older, he required less and less prompting and began to love the piano. His abilities grew exponentially. As an adult, Beethoven himself recalled his early abilities in a letter saying: "I never had to learn to avoid errors . . . for from my childhood I had so keen a sensibility that I wrote correctly without knowing that it had to be so, or could be otherwise." (B, 15) The mature Beethoven explains that he never understood why he, rather than others, had the ability to create art: "Art! Who comprehends her? With whom can one consult concerning the great goddess?" (FK, 13) Later we find this remarkable statement concerning his creative ability:

> *You will ask me where I get my ideas. That I cannot tell you with certainty; they come unsummoned, directly, indirectly,—I could seize them with my hands,—out in the open air; in the woods; while walking; in the silence of the nights; early in the morning; incited by moods, which are translated by the poet into words, by me into tones that sound, and roar and storm about me until I have set them down in notes.* (FK, 29)

Beethoven was convinced that art was eternal, and that the primary source of all art and beauty was the eternal Being of God. Robert Haven Schauffler points out that in his letters Beethoven speaks of being "'impelled' as though by some external force to create."

Like the Romantics, which he loved to read, Beethoven saw evidence of Divine order, beauty, and art in Nature itself. "I spend all my mornings with the muses" he wrote, "and they bless me also in my walks." (FK, 71) Friedrich Kerst says that "The concepts Nature and Art were intimately bound up in [Beethoven's] mind." Like all true sons of the Rhine, Beethoven loved nature. As a young boy he took nature walks, sometimes extended day trips with his father. "Out in the woods," says Kerst, "he became naively happy; to him the woods were a Holy of Holies, a Home of the Mysteries." Indeed, Beethoven wrote a poem recounting these sentiments:

> *Almighty One*
> *In the woods*
> *I am blessed.*
> *Happy every one*
> *In the woods.*
> *Every tree speaks*
> *Through Thee.*
> *O God!*
> *What glory in the*
> *Woodland.*
> *On the Heights*
> *is Peace,—*
> *Peace to serve Him—*
> (FK, 16)

In 1798, Beethoven began to have hearing difficulties which would persist and worsen until his death. He again retreated to Nature for healing:

> *My miserable hearing does not trouble me here. In the country it seems as if every tree said to me: "Holy! holy!"—Who can give complete expression to the ecstasy of the woods! O, the sweet stillness of the woods.* (FK, 17)

The precise cause of his deafness is unknown. Beethoven accepted it as a "decree of Fate." Schauffler points out that the affliction was felt as tragic. Certainly a tragic note in his music began about this time. Schauffler is convinced that out of this period, Beethoven produced the "most sublimely heartbreaking music the world had yet heard: the

Largo e mesto of the D major piano sonata (Op. 10, No. 3), the first part of the *Sonate Pathtique* (Op. 13), and the *Adagio affettuoso appassionato* of the first quartet (Op. 18), which he himself associated with the tomb scene in *Romeo and Juliet*."

The greatest tragedy resulting from his affliction, was his growing reclusive nature. He was embarrassed by his deafness, and retreated from public view whenever he could. In his famous "Heilgenstadt Testament," written to his brothers, Beethoven speaks of his feelings:

> *From my childhood onward my heart and soul have been filled with tender feelings of goodwill . . . But reflect, for the past six years I have been in an incurable condition made worse by unreasonable doctors. . . . Although born with a fiery and lively temperament, and even fond of the distractions of society, I soon had to cut myself off and live in solitude. When, occasionally, I decided to ignore my infirmity, ah, how cruelly I was then driven back by the doubly sad experience of my poor hearing, yet I could not find it in myself to say to people: 'Speak louder, shout, for I am deaf." Ah, how could I possibly have referred to the weakening of a sense which ought to be more perfectly developed in me than in other people, a sense which I once possessed in the greatest perfection . . . . I cannot do it, so forgive me if you see me withdraw from your company, greatly though I should like to mix with you. (BE, 21).*

But while his deafness negatively impacted his relations with people, it may have had a positive affect on his music. During the same time the "Testament" was written, Beethoven's creative work continued: the Second Symphony, the three Violin Sonatas (Op. 30), the three Piano Sonatas (Op. 31), and other were all written during this time. Perhaps most celebrated is the Third Symphony (Op. 55), known as "Eroica," which was originally written as a tribute to Napoleon (though his feelings towards Napoleon changed when he became the self-declared "Emperor").

Schauffler goes so far as to say that Beethoven's deafness "freed" his music: "It is hard to overestimate the gain which resulted for music from Beethoven's deafness. It weaned him away from the distractions of piano virtuosity . . . . It threw him wholly into composition. So, by chance, Beethoven provided an example which freed creative music from the evil old tradition that composer and interpreter should be one and the same person. . . . Thus he prepared the way for non-virtuoso composers like Berlioz, Schumann, Wagner, Ravel, and Stravinsky." Schauffler suggests another way in which Beethoven's deafness "freed" his music. The compositions no longer needed to include pieces merely to advertise Beethoven's superior dexterity at the keyboard. The composition could reveal the "art on a basis of music for music's sake." Schauffler concludes: "In struggling free of outer compulsion, and writing the bulk of his work from inner compulsion alone, and without regard to consideration of virtuosity, he signed music's declaration of independence."

Beethoven's temperament and attitude towards his "superiors," was far different from Mozart's. Mozart was somewhat stifled by the controls placed upon him from the Archbishop of Salzburg. Beethoven was the first to consider the artist to be above his superiors. The famous story is told that while walking with the famed Goethe, the two men approached a member of royalty; Goethe gave way and bowed, expressing the proper courtesy; Beethoven, on the other hand, scolded Goethe saying "Keep as you are, they must give way to us, not we to them." (S, 314) Goethe, Germany's poet genius, was chilled by Beethoven's attitude and arrogance, broke off any further relationship, and wrote about Beethoven's "utterly untamed personality." (S,316)

Beethoven died on March 26, 1827. Shortly before his death he wrote

> . . . *Indeed, a hard lot has fallen upon me! But I resign myself to the will of destiny, and only ask God constantly to grant through His divine will that, so long as I must still suffer death in life here, I am protected from penury. This will give me the strength to bear my lot, however hard and grievous, with resignation to the will of the Almighty."* (BE, 254).

Reportedly, at his death he uttered these words, "Plaudite, amici, comoedia finia" (Applaud, friends, the comedy is ended). (BE, 254) Unlike the case of Mozart, whose funeral was sparsely attended, Beethoven's burial was marked by all of Vienna. The schools were closed, and the military were called out to control the crowd of twent thousand. He was buried near Mozart. Over his grave lies the bronze symbol of creative genius—a serpent biting its own tail.

Selected Bibliography for Chapter Ten

Blom, Eric: Editor, *Mozart's Letters*. Penguin Books, Baltimore, Maryland, 1968.

Burk, John N.: *The Life and Works of Beethoven*. Modern Library, New York, 1943. Abbreviated (B).

Holmes, Edward: *The Life of Mozart*. J.M. Dent & Sons Ltd., New York, 1939.

Kerst, Friedrich: Beethoven: *The Man and the Artist Revealed in His Own Words*, Henry Krehbiel (trans). Dover Publications, New York, 1964. Abbreviated (FK)

Kerst, Friedrich: *Mozart: The Man and the Artist Revealed in His Own Words*, Henry Krehbiel (trans.). Dover Publications, New York, 1965. Abbreviated (K).

Lang, Paul Henry: Editor, *The Creative World of Mozart*. W.W. Norton, New York, 1963. Abbreviated (L).

Sadie, Stanley: *Mozart*. Grossman Publishers, New York, 1965.

Schauffler, Robert Haven: *Beethoven: The Man Who Freed Music*. Doubleday, New York, 1929. Abbreviated (S).

Schmidt-Gorg, Joseph: *Ludwig Van Beethoven: Bicentennial Edition (1770-1970)*. Duetsche Grammophon Gesellschaft MBH, Hamburg, 1970. Abbreviated (BE).

Chapter 11

Emily Dickinson: A Poetic Genius Looks at Death

Emily Dickinson (1830-1886) was an American poet of incontestable genius who, as Richard Sewall has said, "looked very deep and saw very clear." Her poems invite us to penetrate life itself, and death as a means towards understanding life. Some have said that she was obsessed with this topic (pointing to a fascination with death masks, for example). It is estimated that a quarter of all of Dickinson's poems deal with death.   Conrad Aiken tells us that "she seems to have thought of it constantly—she died all her life, she probed death daily. 'That bareheaded life under grass worries one like a wasp,' she wrote. Ultimately, the obsession became morbid."   Henry Wells, on the other hand, has argued that "there is remarkably little morbidity" in Dickinson's death poems. "Death," he continues, "became for Emily the supreme touchstone for life."   Other scholars agree with Wells.   Richard Wilbur, for example, remarks that Dickinson's contemplations on death are really an attempt to look at life "from the vantage of the grave."   And Genevieve Taggard, in her marvelous book about Dickinson's life, has said that "she saw Death's value. He should be her focus; not her woe."

According to this view, then, Dickinson should not be seen as obsessed with death but with life itself insofar as it can be understood from the grave.   "A Death blow is a Life blow to Some," she writes [P, #816]. As Wells argues, "Death becomes a gateway to vitality, lifelessness to life.   The ultimate of the positive hinges upon the ultimate of the negative. . . .Emily outstares death: she looks so intently and piercingly upon it that its terrors vanish, as fog before the sun. . . . To Emily, death ceases to be a mere theme or problem and becomes the key to art, to beauty, and to life. . . . Death becomes for Emily the mountain of vision.   Like the highest summit in a range, it commands the panorama of the whole. . . . Since for Emily, at least, death is symbol of reality, it becomes not the bitter dead-end of the grave—though on one level it remains that—but the gateway to reality and hence to life, joy, and ecstasy."

And Emily Dickinson did find ecstasy in life. She once told T.W. Higginson (who later, along with

Mabel Loomis Todd, became her first editor) that "I find ecstasy in living—the mere sense of living is joy enough." [L, #342A]. She begins a poem with "Water, is taught by thirst" [P, #135]; and in paraphrasing this we can argue that her contemplations on the mysteries of death were motivated by the belief also that life is taught by death. In a letter she writes that "Life is death we're lengthy at, death the hinge to life" [L, #281]. And we can imagine her speaking of life itself when she says in a poem, "I see thee better—in the Dark—. . . /And in the Grave—I see Thee best—" [P, #611]. "This Conciousness that is aware" she also writes, ". . . Will be the one aware of Death" [P, #822]. Death, then, is not simply a terror to be feared; "So give me back to death/The Death I never feared . . ." [P, #1632], it is also our teacher. Through this dark prism Emily Dickinson, in Sewall's words, "tells us again and again what it's like to be alive."

In this respect, Dickinson bears similarity to Heidegger who taught that the human being is a "*Sein sum Tode*"—a being towards death. But she is also like Marcel in recognizing that it is the very essence of love, in reaching out towards the other, to deny death of our loved ones. She writes, for example, "Unable are the Loved to die/For Love is Immortality,/Nay it is Deity" [P, #809].

And Emily Dickinson loved deeply. One need only look to her many letters wherein she expresses her love, and also her need to be loved. It is true that she became very reclusive, but she never stopped loving. Some would have it that it was an unrequited love that led to the seclusion. But for a more complete picture one has to dig deeper than this into Dickinson's tortured psyche. For she was a lonesome soul, like the Kierkegaard, who praised the need for solitude. "The Soul selects her own Society," she says in a famous poem [P, #303]. But like Nietzsche, she rejected the religious answers to life's mysteries. She refused (to the frustration of her very prominent and Puritan family at Amherst, Massachusetts) to be among "the elect" of God. And again like Nietzsche (who spent his last years in mental collapse), she lived near the boundaries of sanity and insanity. She seemed odd to many. Higginson referred to her as "partially cracked" [L, p. 570]. Upon meeting her face to face for the first time, he remarked that "I never was with any one who drained my nerve power so much. Without touching her, she drew from me" [L, p. 476]. And later, on recalling the meeting in the *Atlantic Monthly*, he writes "The impression made upon me was that of an excess of tension, and of abnormal life. . . . She was much too enigmatical a being for me to solve in an hour's interview . . ." [L, p. 476].

Dickinson was enigmatic. She exhibited strange behavior during this and the rest of her life as a recluse. Upon receiving guests she would rarely reveal herself face to face, preferring to converse between walls or in doorways hidden and half-hidden. In her letters she would ask for understanding. "Pardon my sanity," she says ironically, "in a world *in*sane, and love me if you will, for I had rather *be* loved than to be called a king in earth, or a lord in Heaven" [L, #185]. In 1862 she told Higginson of "a terror—since September—I could tell to none—and so I sing, as the Boy does by the Burying Ground— because I am afraid" [L, #261]. In 1864 she writes of mental collapse in a poem: "I felt a Cleaving in my Mind—/As if my Brain had split—/I tried to match it—Seam by Seam—/But could not make them fit" [P, #937]. And there are many other references in her poetry, if they be taken as autobiography, to her mental troubles: "My Life had stood—a Loaded Gun—" [P, #754]; "I lived on Dread—" [P, #770]; "I've dropped my Brain—My Soul is numb—" [P, #1046]. In 1884 she suffered a nervous breakdown which was to trouble her during the last two years of her life (she died in 1886 of Bright's disease, a kidney ailment). But while these individual moments of mental darkness are no doubt important, still it is true that Emily had always been a troubled spirit. As early as 1852 she wrote "when nobody sees, I brush away big tears with the corner of my apron" [L, #85].

It is that troubled spirit which seems to have given birth to her art. Nietzsche wrote that "one must still have chaos in oneself to be able to give birth to a dancing star." Dickinson spoke of the "Vesuvius at Home" [P #1705] to signal her own inner chaos. "On my volcano grows the Grass," she writes [P, #1677]. According to Adrienne Rich, "Vesuvius at Home is how she perceived herself . . . It's the potential for chaos." Joyce Carol Oates agrees and adds that "It's also the Vesuvius that drives VanGogh insane. It's also the dark night of the soul." Dickinson seemed strangely attracted to darkness rather than to light. "Night is my favorite Day" she says in a letter [L, #843]. And many of her references to light reveal painful images (some have suggested an optical ailment as a possible cause for this).

Dickinson's inner chaos made her painfully aware of a potential danger to her soul. She remarked to Higginson that she had "no Monarch in my life, and cannot rule myself, and when I try to organize—my little Force explodes—and leaves me bare and

charred" [L, #271].   And when he first suggested that
she delay publishing her work, thinking it a little
"wayward,"   she   wrote   "You   think   my   gait
'spasmodic'—I   am   in   danger—Sir—/You   think   me
'uncontrolled'—I have no Tribunal" [L, #265].

So Emily Dickinson faced the chaos within
herself. In having no tribunal, as Sewall remarks, she
was able to write "for herself, and therefore she was
free." Only several of her poems were published in
her lifetime; and then, only anonymously. She hid
her poems away. No one, not even Higginson, was
aware of the volumes of work she was stowing away in
her private room. She instructed her sister Lavinia to
destroy her papers after she died—the great Roman
poet Virgil (70-19 B.C.), had given the same
instructions regarding his classic *Aeneid*. And when
"Vinnie" (as Dickinson preferred to call her) began to
take up the task, she was overwhelmed with what she
found. Thankfully for the world she disobeyed the
dying wish. Dickinson's art soon became known to
the world. No doubt this was her true desire. She
once remarked to Higginson that not publishing her
work would be as "foreign to my thought, as
Firmament to Fin—. If fame belonged to me, I could
not escape her . . . "[L, #265]. It seems fitting that one
who sought so much from death, would receive fame
only after she had passed through its door. We who
are still alive are the benefactors. We who have not
yet succumbed to the dark night stand ready to
receive the truth from her art.

We begin with a poem which, in talking about
death, links art and truth together in a style
reminiscent of Keats' "Ode on a Grecian Urn"—

"Beauty is truth, truth beauty,—that is all/Ye know on earth, and all ye need to know."

I died for Beauty—but was scarce
Adjusted in the Tomb
When One who died for Truth, was lain
In an adjoining Room—

He questioned softly "Why I failed"?
"For Beauty", I replied—
"And I—for Truth—Themself are One—
We Brethren, are", He said—

And so, as Kinsmen, met a Night—
We talked between the Rooms—
Until the Moss had reached our lips—
And covered up—our names—
[P, #449]

In reading this poem one can almost "feel" the act of dying. It is as if we are brought to death's door; it standing open and revealed with stark realism. One can only read with awe and wonder, and ask how anyone can have experienced the reality of death so crisply. And how is it that we, the living readers of this poem, are able to recognize these unmistakable ciphers of death? Is it because we, who still participate in life, are somehow aware of life's opposite? Is it because those still in the light are able to detect the nature and quality of darkness?

And what of the connections that Dickinson seems to be drawing between beauty and truth ("Themself are One")? Plato, too, links beauty and truth (as well as goodness) together. Beauty and truth, he taught, must finally collapse into goodness as the ultimate reality.

Beside these philosophical conundrums, there lies the real value of the death poem—it brings us there to feel the truth for ourselves. It is an example of what Kierkegaard called "subjective truth": a truth to be passionately felt. And while the ultimate point may be to look more closely at life, still there is no reducing the real horrors of death. Dickinson faces death squarely and eye-to-eye.

Safe in their Alabaster Chambers—
Untouched by Morning—
And untouched by Noon—
Lie the meek members of the Resurrection—
Rafter of Satin—and Roof of Stone!

Grand go the Years—in the Crescent—above them—
Worlds scoop their Arcs—
And Firmaments—row—
Diadems—drop—and Doges—surrender—
Soundless as dots—on a Disc of Snow—
[P, #216, version of 1861]

One difference between this and poem #449, is that it is cast in the third person. In 449, Dickinson imagines the experience of death in the first person; in 216 she speaks about the death of others. Another difference is the introduction of the element of safety: "Safe in their Alabaster Chambers"—how ironic that true safety only comes when we are in the tomb. But safe from what? She seems to mean that we are safe from the daily troubles which life usually brings us— we are "untouched" by "Morning" and "Noon". A key similarity between the two poems is that both end with the unavoidable and undeniable reality of silence: "We talked between the Rooms—/Until the Moss had reached our lips—/And covered up—our names—" (449); and "Diadems drop—and Doges—surrender—/Soundless as dots—on a Disc of Snow—" (216). Such reference to silence or stillness is a common theme found in Dickinson's death poems. "I heard a Fly buzz—when I died—" she writes, "The Stillness in the Room/Was like the Stillness in the Air—/Between the Heaves of Storm" [P, #465]. But the silence in 216 brings a freedom: "Diadems drop,"—diadems comes from the Greek for "bound up" as with a rope. She seems to be saying that in death we are no longer bound up by the troubles of life. And it brings a surrender: "Doges surrender,"—doges comes from the Latin for "leaders." In death, there are no leaders except death itself, to which all must surrender. Even when we try to avoid death, it finds us, as she reveals in another poem: "Because I could not stop for Death—/He kindly stopped for me—" [P, #712].

I felt a Funeral, in my Brain,
And Mourners to and fro
Kept treading—treading—till it seemed
That Sense was breaking through—

And when they all were seated,
A Service, like a Drum—
Kept beating—beating—till I thought
My Mind was going numb—

And then I heard them lift a Box
And creak across my Soul
With those same Boots of Lead, again,
Then Space—began to toll,

As all the Heavens were a Bell,
And Being, but an Ear,
And I, and Silence, some strange Race
Wrecked, solitary, here—

And then a Plank in Reason, broke,
And I dropped down, and down—
And hit a World, at every plunge,
And Finished knowing—then—
[P, #280]

Here we revert back to the first person. The focus is on the sensory experience of death itself, highlighting "Sense," "Mind," "Space," "Silence," "Reason," and "knowing". Dickinson feels the sensations of death, and she feels the silence of empty space as well. Paradoxically, she hears that silence : "Then Space—began to toll,/As all the Heavens were a Bell,/And Being, but an Ear". But the senses are breaking down, and so is reason: "And then a Plank in Reason, broke." And we are left not only in silence, as in poems 216 and 449, but with the end of knowledge: "And Finished knowing—then—." Dickinson does not attempt to disguise the realities of death. She seems to be saying here, like the philosopher Epicurus (341-271 B.C.), that death signals the end of the feeling, sensing, knowing subject.

Is this not a view of death as unconquerable? Is there no hope for an afterlife? We have already seen Dickinson's rejections of her family's religion. And in another poem she hints at the failure of religion to overcome the finalities of death: "Much Gesture, from the Pulpit—/Strong Hallelujahs roll—/Narcotics cannot still the Tooth/That nibbles at the soul—" [P, #501]. She also writes that "No Drug for Consciousness—can be—/Alternative to die/Is Nature's only Pharmacy/For Being's Malady—" [P, #7L6].

But what do the death poems really teach us about life? How does this darkness cast light? The hint, perhaps, comes with the following poem:

Of Death I try to think like this—
The Well in which they lay us
Is but the Likeness of the Brook
That menaced not to slay us,
But to invite by that Dismay
Which is the Zest of sweetness
To the same Flower Hesperian,
Decoying but to greet us—

I do remember when a Child
With bolder Playmates straying
To where a Brook that seemed a Sea
Withheld us by its roaring
From just a Purple Flower beyond
Until constrained to clutch it
If Doom itself were the result,
The boldest leaped, and clutched it—
[P, #1558]

Here death is seen not as the "menace," but rather as that which "invites" us. Invites us where and to do what? To the "Flower Hesperian" (the evening flower); to the "Zest of sweetness" (is this not life itself?). The "boldest" among us leap to clutch at the flower of life. Death disguised ("decoying") as a "roaring" "Sea," is there "to greet us" and to provide that obstacle to overcome.

Dickinson's ideas here resemble Nietzche again. He wrote of the "overman" (*übermensch*)—the one who becomes the master over one's own life—the overman overcomes obstacles, and death is the ultimate obstacle. Dickinson's notion of death as the roaring sea is also reminiscent of Nietzsche's view that our lives lie before us like an open sea. "The sea, our sea, lies open again;" he wrote, "perhaps there has never yet been such an 'open sea'." The boldest ones are like Nietzsche's overman—they leap and clutch death. In doing so, they affirm life. And so we end with a poem about that affirmation.

The Props assist the House
Until the House is built
and then the Props withdraw
And adequate, erect,
The House support itself
And cease to recollect
The Auger and the Carpenter—
Just such a retrospect
Hath the perfected Life—
A past of Plank and Nail
And slowness—then the Scaffolds drop
Affirming it a Soul
[P, #1142]

This poem can be read within the context of the death poems we have examined. The "Props" which assist us in our self-development represent family, religion, society, culture—all that which nurtures us, but which also disguises, through various myths, the realities of death. Self realization and actualization ("The House support itself") require that we allow that the "Props withdraw" and "Scaffolds drop." In allowing this we do not reject them entirely, nor our love for them—there simply is no need to lean on them anymore. In facing death we affirm our own souls and stand "adequate, erect" towards life.

Selected Bibliography for Chapter Eleven

Aiken, Conrad: "Emily Dickinson," in *Emily Dickinson: A Collection of Critical Essays*, R. Sewall (ed.), Prentice Hall, Englewood Cliffs, pp. 9-15, 1963.

Barker, Wendy: *Lunacy of Light: Emily Dickinson and the Experience of Metaphor*, Southern Illinois University Press, Carbondale, 1987.

Benfey, C. E. G.: *Emily Dickinson and the Problem of Others*, University of Massachusetts Press, Amherst, 1984

Bretall, R. (editor): *A Kierkegaard Anthology*, Modern Library, New York, 1946.

Dryden, J. (trans.): *Virgil's Aeneid*, Harvard Classics Volume 13, P.F. Collier And Son, New York, 1969.

Epicurus, "Letter to Menoeceus," in *Letters, Principal Doctrines, and Vatican Sayings*, R. M. Geer (trans.), Library of Liberal Arts, Indianapolis, 1964.

Heidegger, Martin: *Being and Time*, John Macqarrie and Edward Robinson (trans.), Harper and Row, New York, 1962.

Johnson, T.H. (editor): *The Complete Poems of Emily Dickinson*, Little, Brown and Company, Boston, 1955. Abbreviated as (P)

————————:*The Letters of Emily Dickinson*, Harvard University Press, Cambridge, 1958. Abbreviated as (L)

Kaplan, J.D. (ed.): *Dialogues of Plato*, Pocket Books, New York, 1950.

Kaufmann, Walter (trans.): *The Portable Nietzsche*, The Viking Press, New York, 1961.

Keats, John: "Ode on a Grecian Urn," in the *Norton Anthology of English Literature*, volume 2, W.W. Norton and Company, New York, p. 532, 1968.

Marcel, Gabriel: *Being and Having*, K. Farrer (trans.), Harper Torchbooks, New York, 1965.

Taggard, Genieve: *The Life and Mind of Emily Dickinson*, Alfred A. Knopf, New York, 1930.

Visions and Voices, episode 3: *Emily Dickinson*. Annenberg/CPB project (PBS Video interviews with Joyce Carol Oates, Adrienne Rich, and Robert Sewall), the Center for Visual History, New York, 1988.

Wells, Henry W.: *Introduction to Emily Dickinson*, Hendricks House, Chicago, 1947.

Wilbur, Richard: "Sumptuous Destitution," in *Emily Dickinson: A Collection of Critical Essays*, R. Sewall (ed.), Prentice Hall, Englewood Cliffs, pp. 127-136, 1963.

Chapter 12

Vincent Van Gogh:
Risking My Life for My Art

   The very last letter Vincent Van Gogh (1853-1890) wrote to his beloved brother Theo contained these fated words: "Well, my own work, I am risking my life for it and my reason has half foundered because of it." (#652)   This letter was found in Vincent's clothes on July 29, 1890, after he died from a self-inflicted gunshot wound in the stomach. He shot himself in a wheat field and walked back to his room where he was discovered by his landlord. He died two days later.

Vincent's last works were, as he described them, "vast fields of wheat under troubled skies, and I did not need to go out of my way to express sadness and extreme loneliness." Robert Wallace points out that in one of Van Gogh's last paintings, *Wheat Field with Crows*, "his anxiety is obvious. In an alarming inversion of perspective, the horizon appears to be rushing at the spectator as though to engulf him; nothing promises hope of escape." (W, 165)

Vincent's words to Theo sound like familiar warnings. His "I am risking my life for it [my art]" is similar to Dickinson's words to Higginson about her poetic work: "I am in danger—Sir." These two creative geniuses share a very similar spirit. They were both troubled souls who felt that their art, in some way, endangered their psychological health. Like Dickinson, who referred to herself as "Vesuvius at home," Van Gogh had volcanic eruptions of creativity—sometimes producing a painting a day week after week. He refers to his own "inner conflict" (#306) and of "an almost unbearable state of wavering and inner struggle." (#345) All this is reminiscent, too, of Nietzsche's famous line: "one must still have chaos in oneself to be able to give birth to a dancing star." Vincent did have chaos within, and he produced many dancing stars. Only ten years of his life was dedicated to serious artwork, the first four of them to drawing only. In the end, we have 1700 surviving works (900 drawings and 800 paintings). He sold only one of his paintings in his lifetime (for

$80). He felt useless and unappreciated. Yet today, he is considered among the great founders of modern art, and some of his works have sold for many millions.

Vincent Van Gogh was born on March 30, 1853 in a Dutch province. His father was an unintelligent Dutch Reformed pastor, and he and Vincent's mother emphasized the bourgeois values (a good paying job, property, and a good outward appearance) that Vincent came to hate. In his adult life Vincent often complained about his father in his letters to Theo. He felt that his father was trying to "force on me as a duty" the rule of life: "Earn money, and your life will become straight." (#347) Vincent was convinced that the opposite was true: one should first strive to live a straight and honest life and the rest will take care of itself; and if not, so be it. After dedicating his life to art he wrote:

> *I would rather have a 150 francs a month as a painter than 1500 francs a month in another position, . . . I think one feels more a man among other men as a painter . . . . I wonder how it will all turn out, but it is all the same to me, one way or another.* (#335)

Vincent was the eldest of the children—he had three sisters and one brother, Theo, who became his soulmate, friend, confidant and supporter. But before Vincent was born, exactly one year before to the day, the Van Goghs suffered a still birth—a boy, also named Vincent. The first Vincent was buried in a grave near the church that Vincent walked past every Sunday of his life as a child. This must have been a very strange and unpleasant experience for Vincent.

Wallace tells us that the dead child's name was often mentioned in Vincent's presence, and it is a possible source (scholars debate) for Vincent's later sense of melancholy and of being "an inadequate usurper." W.H. Auden says that this situation "may have caused an unconscious inner guilt." (A, 7)

Yet, Vincent's childhood was not always marked by dark broodings. He was, in fact, a happy and charming young boy. His siblings enjoyed his company and the many games he invented for them. At 12, after his father was convinced that Vincent was becoming unruly and influenced by neighboring peasant boys, he was sent to boarding school in Zevenbergen where he read the works of Shakespeare, Keats, Voltaire, Homer, and Dickens. At 16 he left school, perhaps for financial reasons, to become a reproducer of famous paintings. At 20 he was transferred to London, where he fell in love with his landlady's daughter. When the woman rejected him, he suffered a terrible blow. He became more and more withdrawn, and his behavior began to worry his family. Vincent's letters became more rare and peculiar. His melancholy was reflected in a quotation from Ernest Renan which he used in a letter to his family: "Man is not on this earth merely to be happy, nor even simply to be honest. He is there to realize great things for humanity, to attain nobility and to surmount the vulgarity in which the existence of almost all individuals drags on." (W, 11)

During the next few years he entered a period of religious fanaticism. At 23 he lost his job due to a carelessness towards his work. At 24 he briefly studied for the ministry. He was not up to the rigors of study and Latin and Greek. He had a failed opportunity as a lay minister to a coal mining town in

Belgium, where he was dismissed for his "excessive zeal." Vincent then began a period he referred to as his "molting time" (#133), wherein he shed his religious fanaticism and turned towards a career as an artist. Theo had previously encouraged him to paint and had always believed in his talent. And when Vincent started his serious career, he began by sketching the coal miners in their everyday settings. Soon he began to focus on peasant workers—he admired them and considered their daily actions far more fitting as a subject for art: "Painting peasant life is a serious thing, and I should reproach myself if I did not try to make pictures which will arouse serious thoughts in those who think seriously about art and about life." (#404) In the same letter he defends his preoccupation with peasant life:

> . . . a peasant girl is more beautiful than a lady in her dusty, patched blue skirt and bodice, [and] If a peasant picture smells of bacon, smoke, potato steam—all right, that's not unhealthy; if a stable smells of dung—all right, that belongs to a stable; if the field has an odor of ripe corn or potatoes or of guano or manure— that's healthy, especially for city people. Such pictures may teach them something. . . . one must paint the peasants as being one of them, as feeling, thinking as they do. Because one cannot help the way one is.

And so the great drawings of peasant life came. Among them were *The Woodcutter*, the *Avenue of Polaris*, and the *Peasant Woman Tying a Sheaf*. From this tradition of peasant life came his later painting *The Potato Eaters*, considered his first great masterpiece.

Vincent was also drawn to nature itself as a fit subject for art. In this respect he is very in tune with Romanticism. Often his words are reminiscent of Wordsworth and Coleridge, as, for example, this advice to Theo:

> *Try to take as many walks as you can and keep your love of nature, for that is the true way to learn to understand art more and more. Painters understand and love nature and* teach us to see her. (#313)

In another letter, he wrote:

> *I cannot understand why everybody does not see it and feel it; nature or God does it for everyone who has eyes and ears and a heart to understand. For this reason I think a painter is happy because he is in harmony with nature as soon as he can express a little of what he sees.* (#248)

And he is aware that it is not always so easy; "one does not paint," he wrote, "to have an easy time of it." (#388b) He recognized that there are "times in our lives when we seem deaf to nature or when nature doesn't seem to speak to us any more." (#237) Yet he was determined: "I shall be a *painter*, I want to *remain human*—going *into* nature." (#347) He, like Nietzsche, was determined to be himself. "Let us paint," he says to Theo, "as much as we can and be productive, *and, with all our faults and qualities, be ourselves.*" (#399) And whether he would have success in finding himself, he was convinced, was not contingent upon whether his work was valued by others, but upon whether he would find nature's secret: "...whether people approve or do not approve of what I do and how I do it, I personally know no other way than to wrestle with nature long enough for her to tell me her secret." (#393)

Van Gogh's view of creativity is reminiscent of that which we have seen in Marcel. Just as Marcel claimed the human creator a "homo viator"—a traveler and wayfarer, on a never ending journey seeking to create meaning, Van Gogh proclaims himself "'an artist'—. . .these words connote 'Always seeking without absolutely finding'." (#192) And just as Marcel argues that the artist is no *ex nihilo* creator, i.e., one who is in complete control and receiving nothing from God or nature, Van Gogh, speaking of his own ability to create a work says:

> *I do not myself know how I paint it. I sit down with a white board before the spot that strikes me, I look at what is before my eyes, I say to myself, That white board must become something; I come back dissatisfied—I put it away, and when I have rested a little, I go back and look at it with a kind of fear. Then I am still dissatisfied, because I still have that splendid scene too clearly in my mind to be satisfied with what I made of it. But I find in my work an echo of what struck me, after all. I see that nature has told me something, has spoken to me, and that I have put it down in shorthand.* (#228)

Van Gogh was clearly aware that creation is an act not just of giving (*ex nihilo*), but of giving and receiving both. The artist receives from the natural world and from God—"I think that everything which is really good and beautiful—of inner moral, spiritual and sublime beauty in men and their works—comes from God," (#133) and then gives back to the human world for our reception and aesthetic enrichment.

Van Gogh was a giving person, and he had a need to love and be loved. He believed that loving itself, was the true path to God: "I always think that the best way to know God is to love many things. Love a friend, a wife, something—whatever you like— you will be on the way to knowing more about Him." (#133) Wallace tells us that "few men have ever had greater capacity to give love, or greater need to receive it"—here is another similarity with Dickinson. But Van Gogh was able to express his love in his art. He signed each painting with the very personal "Vincent" as if, according to Wallace, he were "sending urgent, affectionate messages to someone, anyone, who might be kind enough to accept him as a friend." He sought out love and friendship, unhappily, with very little return (his brother Theo was the exception). He had several failed relationships with women—we have spoken of one rejection, and there were others to follow. He did finally take up with a prostitute named Sien, who became his mistress for more than one year. After their relationship ended he returned to countryside painting, and she to a brothel.

Van Gogh sought out friendships among fellow artists, as well. This, too, led to unhappy endings. He had naive hopes to start an artist's commune at his small yellow (his favorite color) house in the south of France. He was eventually able to coax Paul Gauguin to come. At first, their relationship was stable—they painted together and discussed art in the evenings. But soon the relationship exploded and became tragic. The two quarreled often, and the quarrels led to attacks. Van Gogh nearly attacked Gauguin with an open razor—later he used the weapon to cut of his own ear. After he stopped the flow of blood and wearing a bandage, Van Gogh's bizarre behavior continued—he delivered the severed ear to a prostitute named Rachel saying "keep this object like a treasure." As Wallace points out, many critics blame Gauguin for this whole affair suggesting that "the cynical, sarcastic Paul Gauguin goaded Vincent Van Gogh to the breaking point." But Vincent's behavior seems to be the almost inevitable outcome of a growing madness, and, today, scholars suggest he suffered from paranoid schizophrenia and manic-depressive psychosis. In calmer days Vincent once wrote that he would never even think of committing suicide (#337). But his madness overcame him. The chaos within snuffed out his ability to give birth to dancing stars. Yet, Van Gogh's creations live on. In his art, we are touched by Van Gogh himself. This is nothing less than the realization of his intentions: "I want you to understand clearly my conception of art," he wrote, "What I want and aim at is confoundedly difficult, and yet I do not think I aim too high. I want to do drawings which *touch* people . . . . I want to progress so far that people will say of my wok, he feels deeply, he feels tenderly . . . ." (W, 33)

The great artist is the one who feels deeply and is able to show those feelings to the rest of us. Vincent Van Gogh fits this definition perfectly, for he certainly felt deeply, and those who are fortunate enough to experience his artwork, also share those deep feelings.

Selected Bibliography for Chapter Twelve

Auden, W.H.: *Van Gogh: A Self-Portrait.* New York
Graphic Society, Greenwich, Connecticut, 1961.
Abbreviated (A). Van Gogh's letters quoted in
this chapter refer to the numbered letters in this
volume.

Meier-Graefe, Julius: *Vincent Van Gogh: A
Bibliographical Study.* Harcourt, Brace and
Company, New York, 1933.

Stone, Irving: *Lust For Life: A Novel of Vincent Van
Gogh.* The Heritage Reprints, New York, 1937.

Uhde, W: *Vincent Van Gogh Paintings and Drawings*
(editor). Phaidon Press, New York, 1941.

Wallace, Robert: *The World of Van Gogh.* Time-Life
Books, New York 1972. Abbreviated (W).

Chapter 13

Oscar Wilde:
The Picture of Dorian Gray

We have encountered some of the ideas of Oscar Wilde (1854-1900) in earlier chapters. We have seen that he was a major leader of the Aesthetic Movement and a proponent of the "Art for Art's sake" philosophy. He showed promise early as a brilliant writer—he won the coveted Newdigate Prize while a student at Oxford. He became one of the most popular literary figures in history, known for his quick and biting wit and wisdom.

He was a prolific writer of fairy tales (*The Happy Prince and Other Tales*); drama (*A Woman of No Importance; The Importance of Being Earnest*); and novels (*The Picture of Dorian Gray; The House of Pomegranates*).   His play, *Lady Windemere's Fan*, brought him wide fame and fortune.

His personal life was not so fortunate. In May of 1895 he was sentenced to two years of imprisonment for the "crime" of homosexuality (punishable under the Criminal Law Amendment Act). The penalty was especially harsh and included unrelenting hard labor. The experience seems to have aged him prematurely. He did publish the poem "The Ballad of Reading Gaol" after his release, which was widely proclaimed. He died in Paris in 1900.

In this chapter we examine Oscar Wilde's wonderful and intriguing novel of 1891.

The Picture of Dorian Gray

Main Characters:

Dorian Gray—The young man who is led into temptation

Lord Henry (Harry) Wooton—The cynical tempter of Dorian

Basil Hallward—The artist friend who paints Dorian's portrait

Sibyl Vane—The young actress who falls in love with Dorian

Brief Synopsis:

Dorian Gray is an angel-faced young man who trades his soul for eternal youth and beauty. Basil's portrait of him, which Dorian hides away, ages in Dorian's stead and reveals all of his hideous vices. And Dorian does "fall" into a world of vice and evil— this is the price he pays for succumbing to the temptation initiated by Lord Henry. Many others pay the price as well; some with their lives. One by one, all who have truly loved and cared about Dorian become his victims. But none is a greater victim than Dorian himself who "in gaining the whole world, loses his own soul."

Reflection and Analysis

Basil Hallward has painted a full-length portrait of Dorian revealing Dorian's "extraordinary personal beauty." Basil is troubled by it, and refuses to exhibit the work. He is convinced that the painting reveals more than the beauty of the subject, it reveals, that is, too much of the artist as well:

> Basil: *I know you will laugh at me . . . but I really can't exhibit it. I have put too much of myself into it.*
> Henry: *Too much of yourself in it! Upon my word, Basil, I didn't know you were so vain; and I really can't see any resemblance between you.*

Lord Henry has misunderstood Basil. Basil does not mean that he has put any of his physical likeness into the portrait—he is aware that Dorian is an "Adonis" and that his own beauty is reserved for his art.

> Basil: ... *every portrait that is painted with feeling is a portrait of the artist, not of the sitter. The sitter is merely the accident, the occasion. It is not he who is revealed by the painter; it is rather the painter who, on the coloured canvas, reveals himself. The reason I will not exhibit this picture is that I am afraid that I have shown in it the secret of my soul.*

These lines are all the more interesting in light of the opening words in Wilde's preface to this book:

> *The artist is the creator of beautiful things.*
> *To reveal art and conceal the artist is art's aim.*

But Basil prefers to remain concealed for a non-artistic reason. He chooses to wear the mask. What he seeks to hide is his almost total absorption in the beauty and presence of Dorian Gray. He goes on to tell Henry that upon first laying eyes upon Dorian, "a curious sensation of terror came over me. I knew that I had come face to face with some one whose mere personality was so fascinating that, If I allowed it to do so, it would absorb my whole nature, my whole soul, my very art itself." Later Basil reveals that Dorian "is all my art to me now." But Basil also reveals considerable self-knowledge (more about this later). He is aware, for example, of the potential dangers that lie before him. And as we shall soon see, he understands what is most important in life, and what is less important.

The key event occurs when Dorian and Henry meet for the first time. Upon this occasion Dorian also reveals some self-awareness. He seems to be aware, in fact, of a foreboding danger, as the following lines indicate:

> Henry: (in typical conceit) *You are glad you have met me, Mr. Gray . . . .*
> Dorian: *Yes, I am glad now. I wonder, shall I always be glad?*

In this very brief initial meeting Henry has already begun to poison Dorian. While viewing Basil's portrait of Dorian, Henry remarks that there is "nothing in the world but youth." Nothing more important and worth living (and dying) for. Influenced by this, and upon looking at the portrait of himself, Dorian grows sad:

> Dorian: *How sad it is! I shall grow old, and horrible, and dreadful. But this picture will remain always young. It will never be older than this particular day of June. . . . If it were only the other way! If it were I who was to be always young, and the picture that was to grow old! For that—for that—I would give everything! Yes, there is nothing in the whole world I would not give! I would give my soul for that!*

With these fateful words Dorian's downfall begins. He is later to discover that on this day forward he is granted his wish. He will not age a single day, while his portrait (which he will soon have to hide away) will show quite clearly the age and disease of Dorian's inner life. Basil is quite startled by Dorian's reaction to the painting and his falling prey to Henry's ideas about the importance of youth and beauty:

> Basil: (to Henry) *This is your doing.*
> Henry: *It is the real Dorian Gray—that is all.*
> Basil: *It is not.*

The next important event in Dorian's life slowly reveals to what extent he has been poisoned by Henry. It all begins in a run-down theater, where Dorian witnesses Sibyl Vane, a beautiful young actress cast in the lead role in *Romeo and Juliet.*

Dorian instantly falls in love with Sibyl. Later it becomes clear that what Dorian has fallen in love with is not Sibyl at all, but her art. Her stage portrayals of Juliet and other characters have an overwhelming effect on him. He tells Henry that she has become a major force in his life—competing with Henry's own influence:

> Dorian: (to Henry) *Your voice and the voice of Sibyl Vane are the two things I shall never forget. When I close my eyes, I hear them, and each of them says something different. I don't know which to follow.*

After a third night of watching her perform, Dorian finally meets Sibyl. Soon thereafter, they are engaged to be married. Dorian invites Henry and Basil for an evening performance. This was to be an important turn for the worse. Dorian sets the stage for them by describing Sibyl's artistry in superlative terms. To Dorian, she is art and life itself; pure and sacred. And in a moment of portentous irony, Dorian says that to them both, "When you see Sibyl Vane, you will feel that the man who could wrong her would be a beast, a beast without a heart." But the fall is to come soon, and Dorian will be the one who wrongs Sibyl Vane. It is he who becomes the heartless beast. The Sibyl Vane which performed that evening, though "lovely to look at," thought Henry, had lost her art. Her performance was listless, artificial, and incompetent. This stunned and disappointed Dorian, who was now annoyed and embarrassed:

> Henry: *She is quite beautiful, Dorian, but she can't act. Let us go.*
> Dorian: (bitterly) *I am going to see the play through. I am awfully sorry that I have made you both waste an evening*
> . . . .
> Basil: *My dear Dorian, I should think Miss Vane ill. We will come some other night.*
> Dorian: *I wish she were ill. But she seems to me to be simply callous and cold. She has entirely altered. Last night she was a great artist. This evening she is merely a commonplace mediocre actress.*
> Basil: *Don't talk like that about anyone you love, Dorian. Love is a more wonderful thing than art.*

With these words, Basil reveals a keen wisdom which is lacking in Dorian—some things are more valuable than art. But Dorian is blind to this. Indeed, it was not Sibyl, but her art which he loved. This becomes clear in his conversation with her after the play:

Sibyl: *How badly I acted tonight, Dorian!*
Dorian: *Horribly! It was dreadful. Are you ill? You have no idea what it was. You have no idea what I suffered. . .*
Sibyl: (disappointed that Dorian did not understand why, since she met him, she will never act well again) *Dorian, Dorian, before I knew you, acting was the only reality of my life. It was only in the theatre that I lived. I was Roslalind one night and Portia the other. . . . I knew nothing but shadows, and I thought them real. You came—oh, my beautiful love!—and you freed my soul from prison. . . . You had brought me something higher, something of which all art is but a reflection. . . . Prince Charming! Prince of life! I have grown sick of shadows. You are more to me than all art can ever be.*

In these lines Sibyl reveals ideas reminiscent of Plato. She had found escape from the *shadows* which *imprison* us all. Dorian had released her. Would he understand?

Dorian: *You have killed my love. . . . I loved you because you were marvelous, because you had genius and intellect, because you realized the dreams of great poets and gave shape and substance to the shadows of art. You have thrown it all away. You are shallow and stupid. My God! how mad I was to fall in love with you. . . . Without your art, you are nothing. . . . What are you now? A third-rate actress with a pretty face.*

In this way, Dorian broke off his engagement with the absolutely stunned and piteous Sibyl. Later at home that evening, Dorian noticed the first alteration in Basil's portrait of him. It showed signs of cruelty. The portrait had changed. Had the wish come true? Was Dorian to remain forever young and beautiful, while the portrait reflected the evils of his soul? There seemed to be no other explanation. Yet, this can be turned into good fortune. The portrait can become a "visible emblem of his conscience," . . . and "a guide to him through life." It could serve as a warning against future evils. Dorian resolved to make amends with Sibyl the next day, and to reject the poisonous temptations of Henry. But this was not to be. Dorian's fate had already been sealed. Sibyl had already committed suicide, and he was to blame. He learned of this only the next day, and after he had composed a letter of apology to Sibyl. And he learned it from none other than Henry, who visited him in order to share the news.

Henry, in revealing the news to Dorian, is more concerned with protecting than consoling him. At first, Dorian feels some responsibility: "So I have murdered Sibyl Vane . . . murdered her as surely as if I had cut her throat with a knife." But there was no remorse—in fact, there was not much feeling at all:

Dorian: *Yet the roses are not less lovely for all that. The birds sing just as happily in my garden. And tonight I am to dine with you, and then go on to the opera, and sup somewhere, I suppose, afterwards.*

But then a hint of fear and danger occurs:

Dorian: *And now she is dead. My God! My God! Harry, what shall I do? You don't know the danger I am in, and there is nothing to keep me straight. She would have done that for me.*

But remorse and fear change into anger and reproach:

Dorian: *She had no right to kill herself. It was selfish of her.*
Henry: *My dear Dorian, . . . if you had married this girl, you would have been wretched. . . . the whole thing would have been an absolute failure.*

Dorian feels one final moment of guilt towards his own insensitivity:

Dorian: (to Henry) *why is it that I cannot feel this tragedy as much as I want to? I don't think I am heartless. Do you?*

With these words, Dorian shows himself to be a prisoner. He has become had. Henry has won, and Dorian shall from now on always listen to him. They go on that evening enjoying dinner and the opera, putting no serious thought to the real tragedy. They have become "spectators of the play" and "no longer actors," as Henry put it. We should remember Kierkegaard and Marcel here.

Basil, who visits Dorian the next morning, is greatly disturbed by his callousness:

Basil: *You went to the opera while Sibyl Vane was lying dead in some sordid lodging? . . . Why, man, there are horrors in store for that little white body of hers!*
Dorian: *Stop, Basil! I won't hear it! You must not tell me these things. What is done is done. What is past is past.*
Basil: *You call yesterday the past?*
Dorian: *What does the actual lapse of time got to do with it? It is only shallow people who require years to get rid of an emotion. A man who is master of himself can end a sorrow as easily as he can invent a pleasure. I don't want to be at the mercy of my emotions. I want to use them, to enjoy them, and to dominate them.*
Basil: *Dorian, this is horrible! Something has changed you completely. You look exactly the same wonderful boy who, day after day, used to come down to my studio to sit for this picture. But you were simple, natural, and affectionate then. You were the most unspoiled creature in the whole world. Now, I don't know what has come over you. You talk as if you had no heart, no pity in you. It is all Harry's influence. I see that.*

Basil once again shows his wisdom. He knows that Dorian has become the "beast without a heart" warned of earlier by Dorian himself. And he knows that Henry is to blame for the change.

Dorian, for his part, attempts to convince Basil that there is nothing to fear in all of these events. One needs only to look to the artistic side of things, he argues:

> Dorian: *And besides, my dear Basil, if you*
> *really want to console me, teach me rather to*
> *forget what has happened, or to see it from a*
> *proper artistic point of view. . . . To become the*
> *spectator of one's own life, as Harry says, is to*
> *escape the suffering of life.*

Think of Marcel's warnings here, against the dangers of spectatorship, and against the view of art as spectatorship.   Dorian seeks to become the spectator. In doing so, he ceases to really participate. He seeks to have, but will continue to be had.   Basil holds out for being rather than having—this is his wisdom. But there is no more hope for Dorian. Even he knows that now.   He comes to recognize that "the future was inevitable. [And that] There were passions in him that would find their terrible outlet, dreams that would make the shadow of their evil real."

Dorian is lost.   There are fewer and fewer glimmers of hope left in his soul; fewer signs of self-awareness and guilt.   He begins to lead a life according to what Kierkegaard called the esthetic stage.   He attempts to bury himself in a life of the senses; in a "new Hedonism" as Henry had called it the first day they met, whereupon one attempts "to cure the soul by means of the senses, and the senses by means of the soul."   It all begins with a curious "yellow Book" which Henry gave Dorian.   A book which Dorian soon describes as "poisonous." It was about a young Parisian who attempts to realize all the passions offered by the life of the senses.   Dorian could not escape the influence of the book.   It seemed to him to foretell the details of his own journey into the senses, which he was now embarking upon.   A journey into the senses would serve to help him escape from the horrible truth.

Dorian's journey leads him to the seedy and shadowy corners of town; to opium dens and other "dens of horror," where he is able to practice the life of the senses to the point of debauchery and degradation. And all who come into contact with him, one by one, become victimized by the poison in his soul. Soon, dark and scandalous rumors are spread about Dorian. Some patrons of the dens refer to him as "the devil's bargain," noting that some say "he sold himself to the devil for a pretty face." Some, like Basil, attempt to save Dorian. But Basil is to suffer the same fate as Sibyl. In an earlier encounter, Dorian refuses to allow Basil to see his portrait (Basil wishes to exhibit it in Paris). But Basil returns to warn Dorian about the scandals being told about him. The rumors set even Basil to wonder: "do I know you [Dorian]? Before I could answer that, I should have to see your soul."

Dorian reacts to this remark, first, by turning white from fear. This is soon replaced by a mocking laugh. Only God can see into one's soul, thought Basil. But Dorian knew otherwise. He chooses to reveal the portrait to Basil, who first reacts with utter disbelief. How can this be? There was no evil in the painting he created; only ideal beauty. But Dorian cries in despair that "each of us has heaven and hell in him, Basil." Think of Nietzsche's two forces here, or of the opposing tendencies of the mind pointed to by Jung. Remember also the duality uncovered in chapter one. Basil's disbelief passes into terror and horror. He begs Dorian to pray with him for forgiveness—for both, surely, have sinned:

> Basil: *I worshipped you too much. I am
> punished for it. You worshipped yourself too
> much. We are both punished.*

Basil would certainly be punished. The price
for seeing into Dorian's soul was death—Dorian
plunged a knife into the back of his neck repeatedly.
Basil was the first and only one to die directly at the
hands of Dorian. All others, had and would die
through indirection: Sybil, Jim Vane (Sibyl's brother),
Alan Campbell (a scientist friend whom Dorian
blackmails in order to get rid of Basil's body). And
others would feel the effects of Dorian's poison, both
directly and indirectly.

Dorian, or at least one side of him, knows the
truth. He is aware, at least unconsciously, that "his
soul, certainly, was sick to death." (It is interesting to
note that one of Kierkegaard's major works was
called *The Sickness Unto Death*.) Dorian's sickness is
caused by his placing beauty above all else. He had,
at least at the moment he sold his soul, loved beauty
too much—like Henry, who later claims "that it is
better to be beautiful than to be good." But Dorian
seems to fade in and out of knowing the truth. One
side of him, again, perhaps his unconscious side,
knows the horror of what he has done, and that
Henry has poisoned him. He knows, at least during
brief moments of realization, that beauty should not
be esteemed above truth and goodness. And he
knows the damage that Henry's views have done to
his soul. Henry even denies the reality of the soul
and believes that ". . . art [has] a soul, but that man
[has] not." Again, part of Dorian knows the truth, and
responds decisively:

Don't Harry. The soul is a terrible reality. It can be bought and sold, and bartered away. It can be poisoned, or made perfect. There is a soul in each one of us. I know it.

Dorian even resolves to save himself, or so he thinks. Henry does not want Dorian to change, nor does he believe it within his or anyone's power to change. Dorian again responds with confidence:

Dorian: . . . *you poisoned me with a book once. I should not forgive that. Harry, promise me that you will never lend that book to any one. It does harm.*
Henry: *My dear boy, you are really beginning to moralize. You will soon be going about like the converted, and the revivalist, warning people against all the sins of which you have grown tired. You are much too delightful to do that. Besides, it is of no use. You and I are what we are, and will be what we will be. As for being poisoned by a book, there is no such thing as that. Art has no influence upon action.*

There is much of interest in this exchange between Dorian and Henry. Does art influence life? Can one be poisoned by a book? These questions are all the more interesting when we look to Wilde's preface wherein he states that "There is no such thing as a moral or immoral book. Books are well written, or badly written. That is all." But which of Wilde's characters is correct—Dorian or Henry? They debate over the relationship between art and morality, beauty and goodness. Basil knew that art must be subordinated to love and goodness. But his influence pales in comparison with Henry's. And what about

Henry's dismissals about the possibility of saving oneself. One question comes to the forefront of Dorian's mind: "Was it really true that one could never change?"

Earlier Dorian told Henry that he wanted to change and to become good. "I began my good actions yesterday," he said. He was referring to his brief relationship with Hetty Merton, a beautiful, simple village girl who fell in love with him, and who planned to go away with Dorian that morning. Dorian chose to "leave her as flowerlike as I had found her," to spare her, that is, the terrible misfortune she would no doubt encounter if Dorian continued the relationship. Was Dorian's motive sincere? Was this an unselfish act? We shall soon see the likely answer to these questions. For his part, in typical cynicism, Henry questions whether the act would achieve its desired end. In fact, quite the reverse will no doubt be the case, Henry argues, because Dorian's love for Hetty, though brief, will have destroyed any chance of her being satisfied with any other:

> Henry: *Well, the fact of having met you, and loved you, will teach her to despise her husband, and she will be wretched. From a moral point of view, I cannot say that I think much of your great renunciation. Even as a beginning, it is poor. Besides, how do you know that Hetty isn't floating at the present moment in some starlit mill-pond, with lovely water-lilies round her, like Ophelia?*
> Dorian: *I can't bear this, Harry! You mock at everything, and then suggest the most serious tragedies. I am sorry I told you now. I don't care what you say to me. I know I was right in*

acting as I did. Poor Hetty! . . Don't let us talk about it any more, and don't try to persuade me that the first good action I have done for years, the first little bit of self-sacrifice I have ever known, is really a sort of sin. I want to be better. I am going to be better.

But sometimes even the devil tells the truth—could Henry be right? Was it only sinful selfishness, rather than goodness, which motivated Dorian's act? After Henry left, Dorian began to ponder these things deeply. Then he determined to end the speculation. There was a sure proof in the portrait itself. He must look at it to find some change for the better. He approached the hidden painting quietly. As he removed the purple veil, the truth was revealed (think of Heidegger's definition of truth=*aletheia*—to be uncovered)—there was no change "save that in the eyes there was a look of cunning and in the mouth the curved wrinkle of the hypocrite." In horror and pain he cried out. Dorian now wrestles with the truth for the last time. Could it be that the painting itself, serving as Dorian's conscience, was now warning him to confess his sins? Was it his destiny to die for his sins? Yet there was no evidence left of Basil's body. But was it his duty to confess and to die?

Three words now occupied his attention: "Vanity? Curiosity? Hypocrisy? Had there been nothing more in his renunciation than that? . . . No. There had been nothing more. Through vanity he had spared her. In hypocrisy he had worn the mask of goodness. For curiosity's sake he had tried the denial of self."

But deep down Dorian knows the truth. Dorian knows he is wearing a mask. But it is too late for him, just as it is too late for his vistims. The mask can no longer be removed.

He resolves to escape confession and death by removing the only real evidence against him—the portrait must be destroyed. He found the knife he used to kill Basil: "As it had killed the painter, so it would kill the painter's work, and all that it meant." But as Dorian stabbed the portrait, he let out a cry "so horrible in its agony that the frightened servants woke and crept out of their rooms." Two gentleman and a policeman passing by in the street below heard the cry. All approached the room in earnest. As they entered they found the portrait hanging on the wall. It was "a splendid portrait of their master as they had last seen him, in all the wonder of his exquisite youth and beauty." On the floor lay a "withered, wrinkled" [and] "loathsome of visage" man with a knife in his heart. Upon examining his rings, they recognized who he was. An old and ugly Dorian Gray lay there before them, dead, and providing an answer to the age-old Biblical question:

What does it profit a man if he gain the whole world and lose his own soul?

Selected Bibliography for Chapter Thirteen

Wilde, Oscar: *The Picture of Dorian Gray.* New American Library, New York, 1962.

Chapter 14

Frank Lloyd Wright: Creative Force of Nature

When Frank Lloyd Wright (1869-1959) was a young teenager he witnessed a tragic building collapse in Madison, Wisconsin which took the lives of nearly forty workmen. This event had a profound affect on him. He began to wonder what caused the accident. He later discovered that the contractor had used faulty construction materials. At that moment he made a personal commitment that any building he would design would be rock solid. In his adult life he fulfilled that promise in spectacular fashion by designing the Imperial Hotel in Tokyo, Japan (1916-1922). It was the only building to fully survive the disastrous earthquake of 1923 which killed more than one hundred and forty thousand people in Tokyo and Yokohama.

The young Wright had been interested in architecture already for a number of years. As a young boy his mother schooled him in basic form and design, using building block toys developed by the famed philosopher-educator Friedrick Froebel. These toys consisted of wooden rectangular blocks, cubes, spheres, and triangles. Mrs. Wright had not only purchased the toys, but had intensely studied the educational philosophy of Froebel which she successfully employed in rearing her children, especially with the intent of making young Frank an architect. In his mature writings, Wright attests to the influence of Froebel's philosophy given to him by his mother:

> Mother's intense interest in the Froebel system was awakened at the Philadelphia Centennial, 1876. In the Fredrick Froebel Kindergarten exhibit there, mother found the "Gifts." And "gifts" they were. Along with the gifts was the system, as a basis for design and the elementary geometry behind all natural birth of Form.
>
> Mother was a teacher who loved teaching; . . . [she] learned that Fredrick Froebel taught that children should not be allowed to draw from casual appearances of Nature until they had first

mastered the basic forms lying hidden behind appearances. Cosmic, geometric elements were what should first be made visible to the child-mind. (T, 19)

The young Wright had learned much about form from this education. He later incorporated this knowledge into visible form in his magnificent buildings—the thin, rectangular, horizontal, Froebel block forms are evident in much of his work. In Wright's emphasis on form, too, one can detect an element of Platonic philosophy, especially in the phrase: "forms lying hidden behind appearances." It is Platonic also, to connect form to mathematical elements, as Wright does in his *Autobiography*: "mathematics in co-ordinated Form is architecture."

His father left the family after a bitter argument with his mother when Wright was 16. Nevertheless, he was greatly impacted by his father. From him, in particular, he learned about sound and music. "He taught me to see great symphony as a master's *edifice of sound,*" Wright wrote. Wright's favorite composer was Beethoven, and he was convinced of an inner connection between music and architecture that Beethoven himself must have experienced:

. . . *Beethoven's music is in itself the greatest proof I know of divine harmony alive in the human spirit. . . .*

When I was a small child I used to lie awake listening to the strains of the Sonata Pathétique—Father playing it on the Steinway square downstairs . . . . When I build I often hear his music and yes, when Beethoven made

*music I am sure he sometimes saw buildings like
mine in character, whatever form they may have
taken then.*

*I am sure there is a kinship here. But my
medium is even more abstract—so kindred
spirits who understand the building are even
more rare than in music. There is a similarity of
vision in creation between Music and
Architecture nevertheless.* (A, 422)

It was from Form and Music—the two great
"gifts," that Frank Lloyd Wright derived his
inspiration. But his greatest source of inspiration was
Nature itself (which embodies both Form and Music).
In the *Autobiography* he wrote that "true FORM is
always organic in character. It is really nature-
pattern."

Wright often commented that Nature must be
studied by anyone who desires to understand
structure, pattern, and form:

*We must study nature, . . . it can reveal
principles, form, design, the inner rhythm of all
being. . . . A genius is a man who has an eye to
see nature, a man with a heart to feel nature, a
man with the boldness to follow nature. (F, 110)*

And elsewhere Wright wrote that

*Nature must signify the only visible body
of God we'll ever see. . . . and in it all lies the
power, the majesty, and 'design' of this whole
affair we carelessly call Life. Out of Nature in*

that sense (interior), you're going to get the meaning of Life—whole—if at all. (O, 130)

No doubt this interest in Nature was another "gift" from Wright's mother who loved nature and often took the children for nature hikes. In his adult life Wright looked upon Nature (as the above quote suggests) as the embodiment of the Divine and Sacred in our world. Here he resembles the Romantic thinkers we have studied. Indeed, Wright includes the Romantic thinkers (in particular, Rousseau, Whitman, Emerson, Thoreau and others) as among his favorite influences. In his personal philosophy he is very much like Rousseau. As Norris Kelly Smith says, "The underlying reality . . . reveals itself to Wright, as it did to Rousseau and the Romantic poets, in the integrated and organic nature of Nature, with whose order man is naturally or ideally in harmony." (S, 127)

And Wright echoes Rousseau's ideas when he discusses the relationship between Nature and civilization:

If civilization could be based on knowledge of the principle of nature, only then would it lead us to the development of character—individuality. As civilization is now, it opposes, insults and violates nature, producing cowards of us all and thinning down the inherent force in us. (O, 29)

These lines are in agreement with Rousseau's concerns that society forces individuals to conform and to cease being themselves. The only solution lies with a society based on nature and the natural condition of humankind. Similarly echoing Rousseau's warnings, Wright argued, as Aylesa Forsee points out, that cities "had become volcanic craters of confused forces, unfit places in which to work, because individuals crowded into unhealthy, artificially-lighted, densely packed cells surrounded by congestion, confusion, and a bedlam of harsh noises. Here they became pullers of levers, pressers of buttons. Slaves of the herd instinct, they were lost as human beings." Wright envisioned a better community in the future, "Broadacre City" he called it, which would be made up of decentralized suburban areas, spread out horizontally:

> *Vertical is vertigo, in human life. The horizontal line is the life-line of humankind. An entire nation will someday be one great free extended city. Its citizens will be living broadly spaced on ground of their own in a free pattern where workers in field and factory, in art and craft, science and education, commerce and transportation, will harmoniously intermingle. Each human endeavor will be related to every other on organic lines natural to all. And human life without waste motion, distraction, dissipation, interference, or imposition will take on new forms—better ways of doing everything.*
> (A, 547)

Broadacre City did not come to fruition in Wright's life time, and perhaps it never will be realized fully. It was offered by Wright as an idea, much like Plato's idea of the Republic. This is the way the world could be, say these great visionaries, if only humankind can learn from its mistakes. Wright did offer a model of Broadacre City in a 1935 exhibit at

Rockerfeller Center in New York City. And along with his visions for Broadacre City, Wright envisioned "Usonian" homes. "Usonian" has its roots in "unity" and "union" and is meant to signal a home in unity with nature and with human nature. The Usonian home was to be "proportioned to the human figure" Wright wrote, as opposed to so many buildings which "make the human being feel rather insignificant— developing an inferiority complex in him . . . ."

> *The Usonian house, then, aims to be a natural performance, one that is integral to site; integral to environment; integral to the life of the inhabitants. . . . Into this new integrity, once there, those who live in it will take root and grow. And most of all belonging by nature to the nature of its being.* (K, 294)

Unlike Broadacre City, the Usonian home did become a reality. Wright designed many in his later years, such as the Herbert Jacobs House (Madison, Wisconsin, 1937), the Hannah House (Palo Alto, California, 1937), the Goetsch-Winkler House (Okemos, Michigan, 1939), and Wright's own home at Taliesin West (near Scottsdale, Arizona, 1938, remodeled through 1959).

The home which most embodies Wright's philosophy of the "natural house," is his masterpiece "Fallingwater." Vincent Scully notes that Falling Water "has always been rightfully considered one of the complete masterpieces of twentieth-century art." It was created for wealthy store owner Edgar J. Kaufmann whom Wright described as "intelligent, cooperative, and appreciative" (traits, Wright believed, not always present in his clients). Fallingwater was constructed on a cantilever system as it extends over and above the stream and waterfall (as opposed to alongside it, as a more timid and less creative architect would have preferred). In the drawing below one can observe a distinct similarity in Fallingwater to the Froebel building blocks that Wright was raised on.

Fallingwater (which contains Frank Lloyd Wright's initials) has been called the best-known private residence in the world (after Kaufmann's death, the family gifted it to the State of Pennsylvania). As Eric Peter Nash says, it "is a culmination of Wright's use of abstract, geometric forms and a mature expression of his philosophy of man's place in nature."

For many, Fallingwater also stands as the supreme achievement of Wright's philosophy of "organic architecture." Organic architecture, as perceived by Wright, was motivated by the belief that created structures should be placed in harmony with their surroundings. As Forsee points out, the term "organic architecture" does not originate in Wright, "but he had evolved a new philosophy about it. 'Organic' really meant a natural pattern with all parts related to the whole, the purpose of the building giving it its character." For Wright, organic architecture was no mere preference of style. For him it stood for something extremely important—"When *organic* architecture finds its way to us" he wrote, "we shall have no such senseless destruction of life as we see going around us now." We have already seen Wright's Rousseauian view that in America, individuals "are all headed for conformity." And he was convinced that we are more and more forced to live in what he called "anonymous boxes":

> *Houses have become a series of anonymous boxes that go into a row on row upon row of bigger boxes either merely negative or a mass nuisance. But now the house in this interior or deeper organic sense may come alive as organic architecture.* (K, 293)

And what does Wright mean by "this interior or deeper organic sense"? For him, the two (organic and interior) go hand-in-hand. Organic architecture refers to an *integrity* in architecture. And "Integrity is," he says, "a quality *within* and *of* the man himself. So it is in a building." This notion, Wright recognizes, is a deep influence from Oriental philosophy:

> *Many people have wondered about an Oriental quality they see in my work. . . . when we speak of oriental architecture, we are speaking of something that is more Oriental than Western. . . . my work is, in that deeper philosophical sense, Oriental.* (K, 298)

In particular, Wright often refers to two separate Oriental influences. First, he appeals to the writings of LaoTze, the father of Taoist philosophy and religion who emphasized harmony with nature and the "within" of reality (internal rather than exterior qualities). Secondly, Wright cites the example of Japanese architecture itself, which he saw as promoting "honest" dwellings (in contradistinction to American dwellings which are "not honest"). Wright quotes in several places the Japanese notion from *The Book of Tea*, that "the reality of a room was to be found in the space enclosed by the roof and walls, not in the roof and walls themselves." Wright was convinced of the idea of "building from inside outward" even before these Oriental influences. They served, however, to reinforce his belief in this principle which he felt, as Forsee points out, "neither he nor Lao Tze created" but was, rather, "eternal and therefore universal."

And Wright was, Like Plato, a believer in eternal and universal principles. And like Plato, he believed these principles derived from an innate source in the mind present already at birth, and that the human person's progress rests upon whether he/she can develop what is already latently there. For Wright and Plato, human progress as a whole depends upon whether we can use these eternal/universal principles in the mind (Plato's "forms" or "ideas"), and reproduce them in the concrete everyday world. John Lloyd Wright (Wright's son) puts this succinctly:

> *When I first worked for Dad, I observed that he was convinced that a Source existed which, by its very nature, produced ideas in the mind that could be reproduced in the world. The rejection of his work by ignorance did not faze him. He concentrated on the intelligence that accepted it.* (S, 25)

Like Plato and Marcel, Wright felt that the principles of beauty are not created ex nihilo. As Forsee points out, Wright believed that these "principles are not evolved or invented," rather, "they are perceived." And Wright echoes Marcel's distinction between the attitude required for the creation of beauty—wonder and participation (the attitude of the artist), and that which stifles creativity—curiosity as found in spectatorship: Olgivanna Wright (his last wife) reports that Wright once proclaimed that "One must learn to distinguish between the Curious and the Beautiful." Elsewhere Wright continues this theme:

> *The basic distinction between the curious and the beautiful, in which culture really consists, will make all the difference between a society with a creative soul and a society with none.* (T, 250)

In the end, Wright agrees with the connection between beauty and truth, as found in Plato and Keats (among others):

Truth. Who then is "conservative" in democracy? Would he not be the man with a sense of himself as at one with truth, seeing truth as his own love of the beautiful? "Conservative" then as he looks into nature from his inner self of his and aims to be true to his own spirit—this is the conservative, normal to America. In this spirit beauty will ever be dear to him. Truth in every form becomes necessary to his spirit and the quest of appropriate form is vital to his happiness. The conservative man looking for Truth as the Beautiful, and the Beautiful as Truth. Wittingly or not, the word beautiful *therefore is to him indissolubly associated with the word* truth. (T, 180)

Wright believed that unless beauty and truth be connected, the fate of the individual and the country are hanging at the balance. And so he poses this serious question for every American:

Must the innate beauty of American life succumb or be destroyed? Can we save truth as beauty and beauty as truth in our country only if truth becomes the chief concern of our serious citizens and their artists, architects and men of religion, independent of established authority? (T, 249-250)

Selected Bibliography for Chapter Fourteen

Forsee, Aylesa: *Frank Lloyd Wright: Rebel in Concrete.* Macrae Smith Company, Philadelphia, 1959. Abbreviated (F).

Kaufmann, Edgar: Editor, *Frank Lloyd Wright: Writings and Buildings.* Horizon Press, 1960. Abbreviated (K).

Nash, Eric Peter: *Frank Lloyd Wright: Force of Nature.* Smithmark Publishers, 1996.

Scully, Vincent: *Frank Lloyd Wright.* Pocket Books, New York, 1960.

Smith, Norris K.: *Frank Lloyd Wright: A Study in Architectural Content.* Prentice-Hall, Englewood Cliffs, N.J., 1955. Abbreviated (S).

Wright, Frank Lloyd: *An Autobiography.* Duell, Sloan and Pearce, New York, 1943. Abbreviated (A).

——————————: *A Testament.* Horizon Press, New York, 1957. Abbreviated (T).

Wright, Olgivanna Lloyd: *Our House.* Horizon Press, New York, 1959. Abbreviated (O).

Chapter 15

Carl Jung:
On Psychology and Art

We encountered the psychologist Carl Jung (1875-1961) in chapter one, where we became acquainted with his ideas concerning the unconscious mind and the concept of the "masks" that we wear. Let us now turn to him and explore other rich ideas we can find in his thinking, concerning psychology and artistic creation.

Of the many followers of psychoanalytic thought, Carl Gustav Jung was clearly the closest to his mentor—Sigmund Freud (1856-1939). And just as one cannot understand Plato without being exposed to Socrates, we shall have to briefly explore Freud's impact on Jung. Their friendship was at first deep and intimate, and Freud had hopes that Jung would carry on the tradition of psychoanalysis after his death. However, this was not to be. While always acknowledging the importance of Freud's contributions, Jung eventually came to disagree with Freud in several key areas. As we will see, it is within these disagreements that the heart of Jung's own theory was formed.

Jung was born in Kesswil, Switzerland in 1875, and was raised in an unusual environment. His mother was neurotic, and his father was kind, but weak and moody. He was exposed to death at an early age, and was raised in a strict and religious atmosphere. His parents separated when he was three, motivated, so he thought, by his own severe illness. Being separated from his mother at such an early age left Jung with a distrust of women that he carried with him for many years. When he was six, he found the body of a man who drowned in a flood, and in fact Jung attended many funerals for fisherman who had perished in the waters near the village.

During his early years Jung enjoyed school and did well, but was not popular with other children. To combat his loneliness, he created an imaginary friendship with a manikin he carved out of the end of a wooden ruler, complete with top hat and shoes. Making a bed for him in his pencil box, the manikin became his "friend" whom he spoke to and shared stories with, concerning his thoughts and events of the day. All of this, of course, was a tremendous secret, and Jung in his autobiography wrote "I consider it the essential factor of my boyhood."

During his teenage years Jung became bothered with school. He became bored with religion class and fearful of mathematics. He found he was able to escape the unpleasantness of schoolwork by faking fainting spells. He kept this up for about six months until he overheard his father worrying about his future. Concerned that he was causing too much stress for his father, he overcame the spells and put all his effort into excelling well at school. Jung worked very hard and entered the University of Basel to study medicine, choosing to specialize in psychiatry. It was in this area that he believed he might find the answers to his searching questions about human nature. Graduating in 1900, Jung went to work under the direction of Eugene Bleuler (one of the pioneers in the area of schizophrenia) and created the word association test which is still used today.

In March of 1907 Jung went to Vienna where he met Freud, the famed founder of Psychoanalysis. The two men became close friends, and Freud soon became hopeful that Jung would follow in his footsteps. In 1909 they traveled together to Clark University in Massachusetts, to deliver a series of lectures on psychoanalysis. Jung maintained the highest regard for the depth and insight of Freud's ideas; still, he could not accept the validity of all of Freud's concepts. In particular, he became convinced that there were deeper levels of the unconscious mind, and that energy other than sexual might be involved in some motivations. Freud at first shrugged this off to inexperience, but later came to realize the very real disagreements Jung would propose.

Eventually, Freud dogmatically insisted on complete adherence to all aspects of his theory, something that Jung was not willing to do. The two parted ways in 1912.

In 1913 Jung experienced an emotional disturbance which led him to a period of introspection, though he maintained his ties with family and patients. Though Jung never fully succumbed to pyschosis, the illness was serious enough to force him to resign his position at the University of Zurich. During this time he delved deep into his own unconscious, and began the task of analyzing his own dreams and fantasies. Many of Jung's patients were also suffering from similar complaints, convincing him that important psychological growth was taking place in the disguise of a neurotic illness.

In 1919, after recovering from the anxiety that would allow him to understand his own life, Jung explored many different cultures and peoples, finding what he felt to be essential similarities among the artwork, myths, and folktales of all societies. He returned to his birthplace and was granted a professorship at the University of Basel, where he remained until his death in 1961.

As we have seen, Jung was in agreement with many of Freud's central concepts, but he disagreed with his mentor in three key areas. These included the nature and features of psychic energy, the levels of the unconscious, and the importance of mid-life over early childhood. Let us examine these in more detail.

Jung felt that the nature of psychic energy (that is, the energy for all psychological actions) was global and undifferentiated, rather than being primarily sexual as Freud had asserted. Jung's energy system was a closed system, so that if more energy was placed into one endeavor, other areas would have less energy available: he called this the *principle of equivalence.* He also maintained that energy not used in conscious activities, could be used by the unconscious. In fact, much of the unconscious energy is used to compensate for conscious actions. For example, an individual may feel small and helpless in his conscious life, but dream about being a gladiator or sports hero at night. In this way, conscious feelings are compensated for by unconscious opposites. Jung believed (very possibly as an influence from Nietzsche) that opposing forces existed within the individual, acting as a motivating energy. Healthy individuals strive for a balance between their conscious and unconscious energies. When too much energy is vested in one area, the other will try harder to make for a transfer of energy to the neglected area: Jung referred to this as the *principle of entropy.* Thus, undifferentiated psychic energy flows from strong to weak areas of conscious and unconscious, and aspects seen in consciousness are compensated for by unconscious opposites.

A second point of disagreement between Jung and Freud concerned the unconscious itself. Jung acknowledged that there was indeed a personal unconscious within all people, much as Freud suggested. However, Jung posited a deeper layer of the unconscious that was common to all of humanity based in a shared ancestry. Jung called this the *collective unconscious*—a storehouse for experiences that all human beings share with one another. For example, almost all people are afraid of falling down, dark unfamiliar places, and snakes. Jung argued that these experiences were detrimental to the survival of primitive humans, and therefore a wariness of these events must be beneficial for survival. Jung believed that a predisposition towards these and other events has been handed down by the same principles of Darwinian evolution that gave the human animal its form and structure. He called the actual psychic imprints *archetypes*, and argued that they are found in all people and cultures. Several of the archetypes were given names by Jung. For example, the *animus* was thought to be that part of the female that gave her a deep unconscious understanding of the male. The counterpart in the male was called the *anima*, which allowed the male to enjoy an unconscious understanding of the female with whom he must co-exist.

Perhaps the most interesting of all archetypes was what Jung called the *shadow*. Similar to the Freudian *id* (and, in turn, to Nietzsche's *dionysus*), the shadow embodied all that was reprehensible, wretched, and negative within us. Like its name suggests, the shadow is the dark side of personality, and always acts in an opposite fashion to conscious actions. Jung describes the shadow in the following way: ". . . the shadow is that hidden, repressed, for the most part inferior and guilt-laden personality whose ultimate ramifications reach back into the realm of our animal ancestors and so comprise the whole historical aspect of the unconscious. . ." (ACU, 266)

The third point of difference between Freud and Jung concerned the importance of the middle and later adult years. Freud postulated five key psychosexual stages of development, ending at roughly eighteen years. In terms of personality development, the first five years were seen as crucial, while the adult years were seen as an inevitable result of that foundational period. Jung, on the other hand, gave considerably more importance to the middle adult years. This *second puberty* was marked by a shift in time orientation, that is, from looking at life in terms of how many years one has lived, to how many years one has left. This new perspective awakens the individual to a more inner, reflective, spiritual side. Money, possessions, striving for power, and other such "outer" experiences are not completely abandoned, but are given considerably less significance compared to knowing oneself, understanding one's culture, and exploring the inner personal side of one's nature. Jung referred to this process as *individuation,* or the period of becoming an individual. This voyage of self discovery can be both fulfilling and terrifying; one must come face to face with the contents of the shadow, and accept the negative side of the personality. In addition, one must attempt to unify the opposites in one's life, so that a balanced and harmonious compromise can result. If this can be successfully accomplished, the individual will have reached the realization of the self, which is the highest and most mature form of mental health in Jungian theory. Considering the difficulties of the journey, this is a state not reached by many people.

Jung on Art and Creation

In Jung's "Psychology and Literature," published in *Modern Man in Search of a Soul,* we find many interesting insights into the nature of art and creation. Therein he argues that psychology is the proper science to examine art and creativity, since "the human psyche is the womb of all the arts and sciences." Jung's ideas are especially enlightening in comparison with the philosophies of Nietzsche and Marcel. While he was most likely unaware of Marcel, Jung clearly read, understood and admired Nietzsche as a pivotal figure in the study of human nature—an opinion shared by Freud. In fact, Jung taught graduate seminars on Nietzsche, and the transcripts from these lectures fill several volumes.

Echoing the notion of duality we have encountered in Nietzsche, and in many other areas, Jung points out that in the artist, this duality is especially keen:

> *Every creative person is a duality or a synthesis of contradictory aptitudes.* (MM, 168)

He goes on to elaborate, at least on some aspects of this duality:

> *The artist's life cannot be otherwise than full of conflicts, for two forces are at war within him— on the one hand the common longing for happiness, satisfaction and security in life, and on the other a ruthless passion for creation*

*which may go so far as to override every
personal desire.* (MM, 169)

The "two forces" that Jung points to here seem
to be one and the same with Nietzsche's two forces;
the *apollonian* desire for order and the *dionysian*
passion. And, like Nietzsche, Jung was aware that
the dionysian side could "override" the apollonian
need for order and personal happiness. The artist,
then, may have to pay a personal price for his "gift":

> *There are hardly any exceptions to the rule that
> a person must pay dearly for the divine gift of
> creation.* (MM, 169)

As Marcel made clear, the artist is not just the
receiver of the gift, he also pays the personal price
and becomes a giver himself. It is the art which works
through the artist and takes him over, in a sense, so
that, as we have seen Marcel explain, freedom must
be understood not as an absolute and total
contribution from the artist (or from any human
being, for that matter), but both a giving and a
receiving. Jung understands this very well indeed:

> *Art is a kind of innate drive that seizes a human
> being and makes him his instrument. The artist
> is not a person endowed with free will who
> seeks his own ends, but one who allows art to
> realize its purposes through him.* (MM, 169)

For Jung, the creative drive emanates from the
unconscious world. And, paradoxically, it is the art
itself which creates the artist:

> *The creative process has feminine quality, and the creative work arises from unconscious depths—we might say, from the realm of the mothers. . . . It is not Goethe who creates* Faust, *but* Faust *which creates Goethe.* (MM, 170)

For Jung, this creative takeover by the unconscious is not unhealthy. On the contrary, it is what truly creates an individual and allows him to speak to others with his art:

> *[The artist] has drawn upon the healing and redeeming forces of the collective psyche that underlies consciousness . . . he has penetrated to the matrix of life in which all men are embedded, which imparts a common rhythm to all human existence, and allows the individual to communicate his feeling and his striving to mankind as a whole.* (MM, 172)

Finally, like Marcel, Jung recognizes that what we are discussing here is a form of "participation" on the level of the "mysterious":

> *The secret of artistic creation and the effectiveness of art is to be found in a return to the state of* participation mystique . . (MM, 172)

Thus, in Carl Jung, we find a theory of the psychology of artistic creation which finds much agreement with the philosophical treatment given by Nietzsche (the duality, the opposing forces, etc.) but also recognizes the Marcellian notion. That is, the artist is not the absolute creator or giver. The artist, rather, receives his art from a source beyond his own private individual self—it arises out of the depths (the collective unconscious) that unite all human beings.

Selected Bibliography for Chapter Fifteen

Cooney, William, and Trunk, Barry: *Ten Great Thinkers*. University Press of America, Lanham, MD, 1990.

Jung, Carl: *Modern Man in Search of a Soul*. W.S. Dell and Cary F. Baynes, trans. Harcourt, Brace, New York, 1933. Abbreviated (MM).

_____: *Archetypes of the Collective Unconscious*. Princeton University Press, Princeton, NJ, 1934. Abbreviated (ACU).

Chapter 16

Conclusion: The Quest for Meaning as an End-in-Itself

"Maybe a big magnet pulls, all souls who want truth."
—k.d. lang

In this text we have journeyed through an historical examination of the quest for meaning (part one), and have seen examples of great creative genius (part two). What can we gather concerning the human quest for meaning? Following the line of reasoning offered by Aristotle in his *Nichomachean Ethics*, I think we can say that our search for meaning is a search for something valued as an end-in-itself. We can pursue other things such as success in business, a healthier life, a better education, etc., all as a means to some other end. It makes sense for someone to ask: "why do you want business success?", or "why do you strive for better health?" These are reasonable and fair questions. The answers are always of the form "I desire X for reason Y." For example, one can answer something like: "I desire these things so that I can better provide for my family and our future." There is always some other end in mind when pursuing these other things. The search for business success, or better health, or better education, etc., therefore, is not a search for an end-in-itself. These things are always means to a higher end.

But the question: "why do you want meaning?" does seem to be a rather strange question. There does not seem to be some other end beyond meaning itself. This would seem to indicate that meaning is a higher value than the others, perhaps it is the highest value of all for the human person. This would mean that human beings want meaning more than any other thing in their lives. And while we all pursue this same end, this does not mean that we are all carbon copies of each other. There are certainly numerous forms of meaning that humans pursue. In religious meaning, people pursue their proper relationship with God. In social meaning, they pursue relationships with others—friends and loved ones. We could also talk about aesthetic meaning, wherein a proper appreciation and experience of art, music, and the aesthetic aspects of life are sought. And we could speak of scientific meaning, which would identify that meaning pursued after by the mathematical and empirical sciences—an understanding of our world and our place in it. There are no doubt many other forms of meaning, but they are all of them a search after meaning itself as an end.

The search after meaning seems to be an inescapable and natural feature of being human. In his classic *Man's Search for Meaning*, Viktor Frankl argues that the "striving to find a meaning in one's life is the primary motivational force in man." But the fact that humans naturally pursue meaning, is no guarantee of achieving it. In fact, experience teaches us that countless people have lived lives without meaning. Could it be that we naturally desire what is impossible or nearly impossible to attain? Could it be that we are like Tantalus in the Greek myth? In the myth, Tantalus is punished by the gods and condemned forever to stand chained in a lake up to his chin. As he reaches down to take a drink, the lake recedes. Clusters of fruit hang from a tree above his head, and as he reaches for them they also recede. All the while a huge boulder lies precariously ready to fall and crush him.

How could we be like Tantalus? The huge boulder lying in waiting can be compared to the impending death all of us will someday experience. The thirst after water and fruit can be likened to the quest for meaning—perhaps it too is unattainable. Perhaps meaning lies just beyond our reach as do the requirements for nourishment in Tantalus' case (thus we are *tantalized*=from the Greek *Tantalus*).

Some might argue that we are indeed like Tantalus and that the search for meaning is in vain. It is my hope, however, that this text has pointed to a different conclusion. In his *Summa Contra Gentiles*, Thomas Aquinas argues that "it is impossible for natural desire to be in vain." This view represents a solid tradition reaching back to Aristotle's view expressed in his *De Caelo*: "nature does nothing in vain." For this tradition, the search for meaning is embedded in human nature, and is evidence by itself that attainment is possible (no natural desire is in vain).

It is my sincere hope that this text makes a positive contribution to the natural desire and quest after meaning. The quest for meaning is a human journey, a human struggle, a human hope. The search itself is what may give us hope—let us continue it forever.

Selected Bibliography for Chapter Sixteen

Aquinas, Thomas: *Summa Contra Gentiles* in Opera Omnia, Vols. XIII-XV, Rome, 1882, reprinted in New York, 1948.

Aristotle: *De Caelo* and *Nichomachean Ethics*, in *The Basic Works of Aristotle*. Edited by Richard McKeon. Random House, New York, 1941.

Frankl, Victor E.: *Man's Search for Meaning*. Washington Square Press, New York, 1959.

About the Author

Dr. William Cooney received the Doctorate in philosophy from Marquette University. He is professor of philosophy at Briar Cliff College in Sioux City, Iowa, where he resides with his wife Candace, and their three children: Terra, Shaun, and Lindsey. He is a past recipient of the Burlington-Northern Faculty Excellence Award, and a Distinguished Scholarship Award from his alma mater. His interests include history of philosophy, ethics, aesthetics, and philosophical psychology.

Dr. Cooney is also author *of Reflections on Gabriel Marcel*, The Edwin Mellen Press; *Ten Great Thinkers* (UPA); *From Plato to Piaget* (UPA), as well as numerous articles in professional journals.